AF413742

The Brownie Book

The Brownie Book

KATE JENKINS

Contents

Welcome to Gower Cottage

It seems like only a moment has passed since Gower Cottage Brownies began. Just over two decades ago, our family was living in Sweden for my husband Rob's job. We socialized by giving dinner parties at home, combining our love of food and Rob's fabulous cooking. I was always consigned to sous-chef, but when it came to desserts, I was in charge. I loved trying out new things, and one of those was brownies. After I first served them, our friends insisted on having brownies for all future parties and they became a staple in our house.

When we moved back to Gower in South Wales, I planned to be a stay-at-home mom and look after our two small boys. It was then that my late father-in-law encouraged me to start selling my family-favorite brownies in the community-run shop in the beautiful village of Llanmadoc—little did any of us know where that would end up taking me. Vacationers to the area soon started raving about the brownies, asking if I could send them by mail. I immediately tested this out, baking a batch of brownies, and devising a cardboard container made from an old beer-bottle box to transport them. I popped the package up to the local post office and posted them back to myself, expecting to receive a box full of crumbs.

A few days later the box arrived at my doorstep totally intact, the brownies tasting as delicious as ever. This was my light-bulb moment; I found a friendly neighbor to help me set up a one-page website, took pictures on my old cell phone, and Gower Cottage Brownies was in business! I set about letting the world know, sending boxes to editors of food magazines, and doing everything

I could to get the word out. I soon started winning awards, and branched out to selling at local farmers' markets. During the first year, my poor husband would raise his eyebrows and make the odd joke about my latest "hobby." Rob's not laughing any more—he gave up his "real job" ten years ago, and now works at Gower Cottage for me!

Gower Cottage is the epitome of a kitchen-table start-up and rural cottage industry. It has grown over the years via word of mouth and now ships thousands of gift boxes of brownies to homes across the UK, as well as supplying astonishing venues such as Wimbledon. In no way was Gower Cottage an overnight success. It took many long hours of baking at the cottage until 3:00 a.m., and trying to juggle school runs. But the loyalty of my customers has been second to none—many of our original customers are still buying brownies from us two decades on.

So I can't think of a better way to celebrate our twentieth year than with a book that allows me to share our brownie creations with you all, and to thank all the people who have helped me along the way. It makes complete sense to offer up our fail-safe recipes, alongside hints and tips that I've been asked about over the years. I also want to encourage everyone to bake great brownies, and show just how creative you can get with just two basic baking pans, one square and one round, and ingredients easily found in your kitchen cabinets.

I hope this book will inspire you to bake some luscious treats for your friends and family. Starting with two simple base recipes— our Original Chocolate Brownie (see p12) and White Chocolate

Blondie (see p78)—you can progress through the chapters, creating a variety of flavors and textures, from straightforward brownie drizzle slices to my ultimate celebration desserts and indulgent brownie towers fit for every occasion. With seasonal fillings and special toppings, layers, and sauces—these are the brownies I would serve you from my own kitchen table. Some of the recipes take a little more time than others, but all are simple to follow. Once you've mastered the original recipes you will fly through this book. The glorious thing about brownies is their adaptability, so play around with flavors and ingredients, adding your own favorite twists and touches to "brownify" recipes to your liking, and build on the creations in this book.

I truly hope you'll dive into these pages over and over: a good book is a messy one, and a great brownie is one that's served up time after time. Finally, I hope that you have fun! Baking is about enjoying, experimenting, and sharing. Never worry about the look of your creations—a dusting of powdered sugar is your best friend—and remember that starting with fabulous ingredients and taking time and care will always create super-tasty results.

From my kitchen table to yours, happy brownieing!

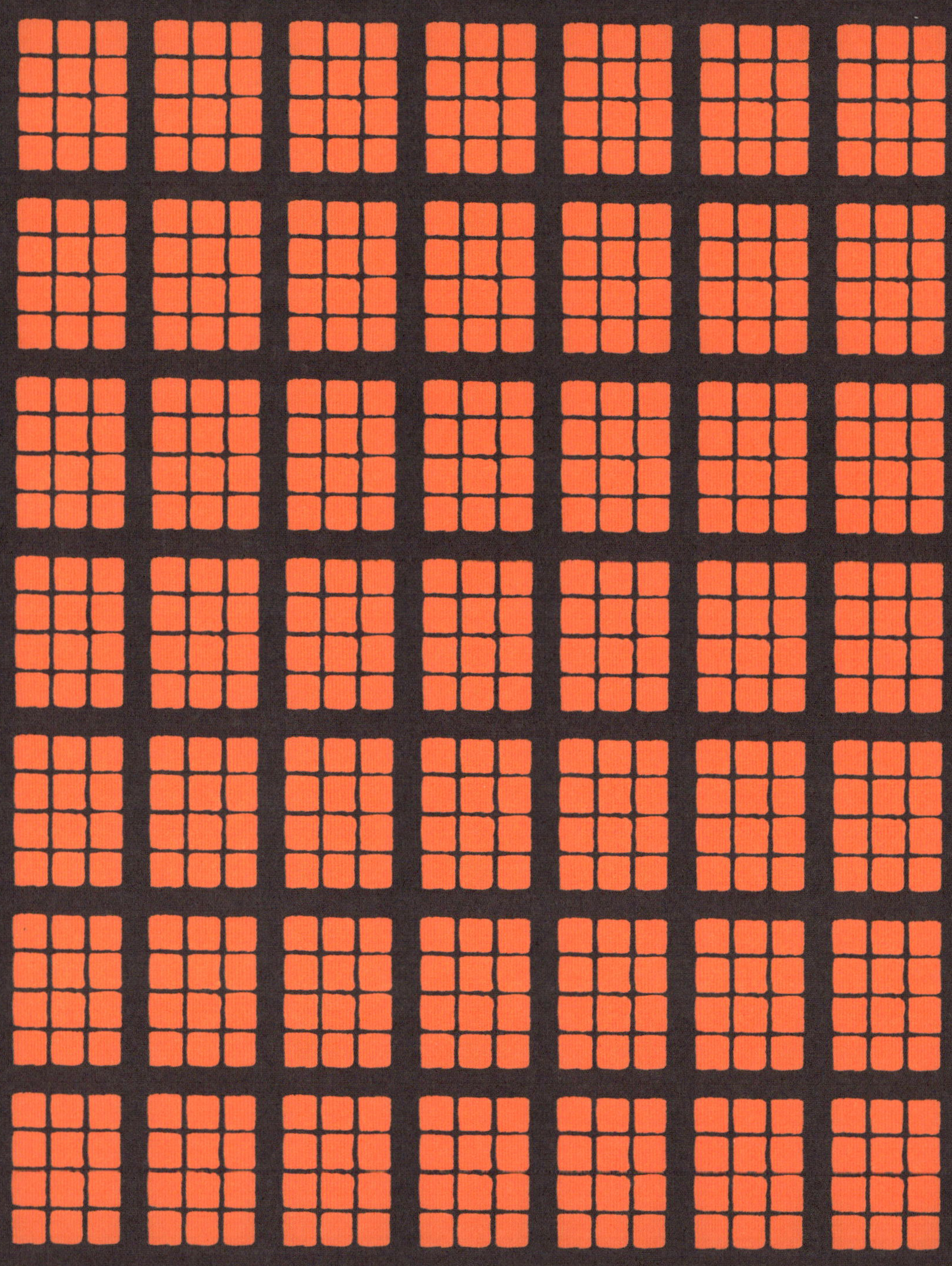

Brownies

The Original Chocolate Brownie

My simple, classic, fail-safe brownie recipe, the original, no-fuss, family pleaser. This recipe is the basis for most of the fantastic brownie creations in this book. Once you've got this nailed, try the Hot Skillet Brownies with your favourite sauce (see right and p79).

MAKES 9

¾ cup (175g) unsalted butter, diced

3½oz (100g) dark (70%) chocolate, broken into small pieces

1½ cups (300g) sugar

½ tsp vanilla extract or paste

¾ cup plus 1 tbsp (100g) all-purpose flour

½ tsp baking powder

3 eggs

YOU WILL NEED

8 x 8 in (20 x 20 cm) square baking pan lined with parchment paper

TIPS

For the best fudgy texture, let the cooked brownies rest at room temperature overnight before portioning up.

If you're in a hurry, pop the cooked brownies in the fridge for 30–45 minutes to cool quickly.

1. Preheat the oven to 350°F (180°C).

2. Put a medium, heavy-based saucepan over medium heat. Add the butter and melt slowly, stirring continuously (be careful not to let it burn). Turn the heat to low, add the chocolate and, using a spatula, keep stirring until the chocolate has melted completely into the butter and you have a smooth, glossy mixture.

3. Take the pan off the heat. Add the sugar and vanilla to the pan and mix thoroughly. Add the flour and baking powder and stir until you have a fine, chocolatey mixture that resembles breadcrumbs, with no lumps of flour or sugar visible.

4. In a medium bowl, whisk the eggs for 20–30 seconds until light and frothy. Carefully fold the whisked eggs through the chocolate mixture, keeping as much air in the mixture as possible, to form a smooth batter.

5. Pour the batter into the prepared pan, spreading it evenly over the base, and bake for 30 minutes. It is done when the edges are set, and the center has risen and started to crack but may still look a bit soft and jiggly.

6. Test with a toothpick. If it comes out completely covered in smooth chocolate, bake for a few minutes more. When it's perfectly cooked, the toothpick should come out with a few small clumps of batter sticking to it. If it comes out clean, the brownie will be more cake-like.

7. Let cool in the pan on a wire rack at room temperature for 1–2 hours to reach the best texture (the brownies will continue to cook as they cool). Slice into 9 equal pieces and serve. The brownies can be stored in an airtight container for 10 days. They also freeze well.

1. Follow steps 1–4, opposite. Pour the batter into a 8 in (20 cm) round skillet or oven-safe dish lined with parchment paper and bake for 25 minutes. The texture will still be soft and quite jiggly.

2. Let cool in the skillet for about 20 minutes (it will be very hot straight from the oven).

3. Serve from the skillet and let everyone dig in, or spoon into bowls. If you like, top with a few scoops of good-quality vanilla ice cream, a few crumbled brownie pieces (from a previous batch), and a drizzle of your favorite sauce (see below and p79).

YOU WILL NEED

8 in (20 cm) round skillet or oven-safe dish lined with parchment paper

Marshmallow Sauce

7oz (200g) marshmallows (all pink if available, or a mix of pink and white)

½ cup (120ml) heavy cream

½ tsp vanilla extract or paste

1. Put the marshmallows and cream in a nonstick pan set over low heat.

2. Stir continuously for 3–5 minutes, until the marshmallows melt and the mixture is fully combined. Add the vanilla and stir again.

3. Let cool slightly before serving.

Hot Chocolate Sauce

¼ cup (50 m) heavy cream

¼ cup (50ml) whole milk

3½oz (100g) dark (70%), chocolate broken into small pieces

2 tbsp unsalted butter, diced, at room temp

2 tbsp corn syrup or honey

1 tsp instant coffee powder (optional)

pinch of salt

1. Heat the cream and milk, covered, in a microwave, for 1½ –2 minutes until it reaches 195°F (90°C). Don't let it boil.

2. Put the chocolate, butter, syrup or honey, coffee powder (if using), and salt in a large heatproof bowl. Pour over the hot cream and milk mixture and use a hand whisk to combine, forming a glossy sauce. Taste, and sweeten with more syrup or honey if desired. Serve hot.

Sugar-Free Brownie

This recipe transforms the classic chocolate brownie into a refined-sugar-free treat, with dates, banana, and honey for natural sweetness. Olive oil replaces butter, while ground almonds and chopped walnuts add rich texture and flavor.

MAKES 9

For the sweetening paste

7oz (200g) pitted dates

1 large ripe banana (about 3½oz/100g), mashed

2 tbsp honey

For the brownie base

¾ cup (175ml) olive oil

4¾oz (130g) dark chocolate

½ tsp vanilla extract or paste

scant ½ cup (50g) all-purpose flour

1 cup (100g) ground almonds

½ tsp baking powder

3 eggs

½ cup (50g) chopped walnuts

YOU WILL NEED

Blender or food processor
8 x 8 in (20 x 20 cm) square baking pan lined with parchment paper

1. To make the sweetening paste, put the dates in a heatproof bowl and pour over boiling water to cover. Let soften for 10–15 minutes.

2. Once softened, drain the dates and add them to a blender or food processor with the banana. Blend until you have a smooth paste. Stir in the honey until thoroughly combined.

3. For the brownie base, heat the olive oil in a medium, heavy-based saucepan over medium heat. Turn the heat to low, add the chocolate and stir until smooth and glossy.

4. Take the pan off the heat. Add the date, banana, and honey paste and the vanilla and mix thoroughly.

5. In a separate bowl, combine the flour, ground almonds, and baking powder. Mix these dry ingredients well, then add to the wet ingredients and mix until well combined.

6. Preheat the oven to 350°F (180°C).

7. In a separate, medium bowl, whisk the eggs for 20–30 seconds until light and frothy. Using a large metal spoon, carefully fold the whisked eggs through the brownie mixture, keeping as much air in the mixture as possible, to form a smooth batter. Fold in the chopped walnuts until evenly distributed.

8. Pour the batter into the prepared pan, spreading it evenly over the base. Bake for 35–40 minutes. It is done when the edges are set, and the center has risen and started to crack (it may still look jiggly). Test with a toothpick. If it comes out covered in smooth chocolate, bake for a few minutes more. When it's cooked, the toothpick will have a few clumps of batter sticking to it. If it comes out clean, the brownie will be more cake-like.

9. Let cool completely in the pan on a wire rack for 1–2 hours. If you're in a hurry, pop the pan in the fridge for 30–45 minutes. Slice into 9 equal pieces and serve.

Gluten-Free Brownie

This is a delicious gluten-free alternative to our classic chocolate brownie, maintaining the desired rich and gooey texture.

MAKES 9

¾ cup (175g) unsalted
   butter, diced

3½oz (100g) dark (70%)
   chocolate, broken into
   small pieces

1½ cups (300g) sugar

½ tsp vanilla extract or paste

scant 1 cup (125g) gluten-free
   bread flour

½ tsp baking powder

3 eggs

1. Preheat the oven to 350°F (180°C).

2. Make the brownie batter, following steps 2–4 of the Original Chocolate Brownie recipe (see p12).

3. Pour the batter into the prepared pan, spreading it evenly over the base. Bake for 35–40 minutes. It is done when the edges are set, and the center has risen and started to crack but may still look a bit soft and jiggly. Test with a toothpick. If it comes out completely covered in smooth chocolate, bake for a few minutes more. When it's perfectly cooked, the toothpick should come out with a few small clumps of batter sticking to it. If it comes out clean, the brownie will be more cake-like.

4. Let cool completely in the pan on a wire rack for 1–2 hours. If you're in a hurry, pop the pan in the fridge for 30–45 minutes. Slice into 9 equal pieces and serve.

TIP

These gluten-free brownies freeze just as well as our regular ones, so keep a batch in the freezer ready for gluten-free guests. They defrost in minutes, or you can warm them through for 20 seconds in the microwave.

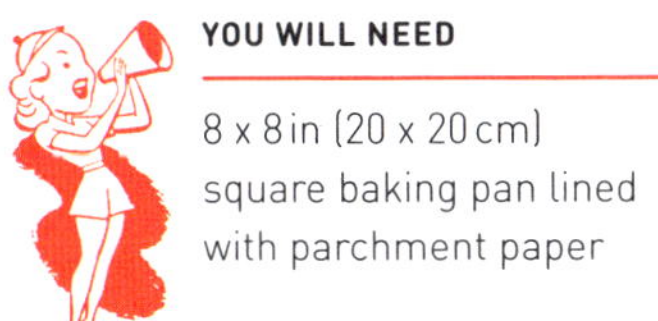

YOU WILL NEED

8 x 8 in (20 x 20 cm) square baking pan lined with parchment paper

Mint Choc Chip Brownie

Imagine an after-dinner mint in the form, taste, and texture of a gooey brownie with added chocolate-chip pieces and fabulous swirls of green running through the whole bake. This is what I've created here. You could also serve these in smaller, bite-sized pieces to enjoy after entertaining friends as a final sweet treat in place of truffles.

MAKES 9

¾ cup (175g) unsalted
   butter, diced

3½oz (100g) dark (70%)
   chocolate, broken into
   small pieces

1½ cups (300g) sugar

½ tsp vanilla extract or paste

¾ cup plus 1 tbsp (100g)
   all-purpose flour

½ tsp baking powder

3 eggs

⅔ cup (100g) chocolate chips
   or chunks

For the mint swirl

4½oz (125g) white chocolate

⅓ cup (80g) sour cream

½ tsp green food coloring

½ tsp peppermint flavoring

1 egg, beaten

1. Preheat the oven to 350°F (180°C).

2. Make the brownie batter, following steps 2–4 of the Original Chocolate Brownie recipe (see p12). When you have folded the whisked eggs into the batter, gently fold in the chocolate chips, reserving one-third to scatter over at the end.

3. For the mint swirl, put the white chocolate in a heatproof bowl, cover, and melt the chocolate in the microwave for 10 seconds at a time, stirring with a spatula each time until the chocolate is smooth and melted. Mix in the sour cream until well combined. Add the green food coloring, peppermint flavoring, and egg. Mix well to form a lovely green mixture.

4. To assemble the brownie, pour half the brownie batter into the prepared pan, spreading it evenly over the base. Carefully spoon half the green mint swirl mixture onto the layer of brownie batter so that you have a separate green layer. Carefully layer the rest of the brownie batter over the mint layer.

5. Gently spoon the rest of the mint swirl mixture on top of the brownie batter. Use a toothpick to swirl the green mixture through the brownie mixture, then scatter over the reserved chocolate chips/chunks.

6. Bake for 40 minutes. It is done when the edges are set, and the center has risen and started to crack but may still look a bit soft and jiggly. Test with a toothpick (see step 6, p12).

7. Let cool completely in the pan on a wire rack for 1–2 hours. If you're in a hurry, pop them in the fridge for 30–45 minutes. Slice into 9 equal pieces or cut into bite-sized pieces as an after-dinner treat.

YOU WILL NEED

8 x 8in (20 x 20 cm)
square baking pan lined
with parchment paper

Bacon Maple Pecan Brownie

We've got it all going on with this one, but trust me, it works. The salty, crunchy toppings cut through the sweetness of the creamy frosting and maple-infused brownie beneath. It seems like a lot more ingredients, but I promise it's very straightforward to put together and is definitely worth it.

MAKES 9

4oz (115g) sliced bacon

⅓ cup (40g) pecans, roughly chopped

2 tbsp maple syrup, plus extra to drizzle (optional)

¾ cup (175g) unsalted butter, diced

3½oz (100g) dark (70%) chocolate, in small pieces

1½ cups (300g) sugar

½ tsp vanilla extract or paste

¾ cup plus 1 tbsp (100g) all-purpose flour

½ tsp baking powder

3 eggs

For the maple bacon frosting

5 tbsp (70g) unsalted butter, softened

scant 1 cup (100g) powdered sugar

⅓ cup (85ml) maple syrup

3 tbsp pecans, roughly chopped, for decoration

YOU WILL NEED

8 x 8 in (20 x 20 cm) square baking pan lined with parchment paper
Electric hand whisk (optional)

1. Preheat the oven to 350°F (180°C).

2. Put the bacon in a nonstick skillet over medium heat, cook until crisp, then transfer to a plate lined with paper towel to cool and drain.

3. Strain the bacon fat from the skillet into a small heatproof container, then refrigerate until firm, reserving 1½ tablespoons for the frosting. When the bacon has cooled, finely chop it and put in a small bowl with the pecans and the 2 tablespoons of maple syrup.

4. Spread the bacon, pecan, and maple mixture over the base of a rimmed baking sheet and roast in the oven for 10 minutes to give everything a maple glaze. Set aside. Keep the oven on.

5. Make the brownie batter, following steps 2–4 of the Original Chocolate Brownie recipe (see p12).

6. Gently fold through three-quarters of the bacon, pecan, and maple mixture until well combined.

7. Pour the batter into the prepared pan, spreading it evenly over the base, and bake for 35 minutes. It is done when the edges are set, and the center has risen and started to crack but may still look a bit soft and jiggly. Test with a toothpick (see step 6, p12). Let the brownie cool completely for 1–2 hours in the pan on a wire rack.

8. For the maple bacon frosting, in a large mixing bowl, use an electric hand whisk (or wooden spoon) to beat the butter, powdered sugar, and reserved bacon fat until well combined, with a smooth, creamy texture. Gradually beat in the maple syrup to make a smooth frosting.

9. Using a palette knife (or the back of a spoon), spread the frosting evenly over the cooled brownie and let it set slightly. If you're in a hurry, pop the pan in the fridge for 30–45 minutes. Scatter over the remaining bacon, pecan, and maple mixture, and drizzle with extra maple syrup, if you like. Slice into 9 equal pieces and serve.

Nut Butter Swirl Brownie

This recipe combines our classic chocolate brownie base with a delicious swirl of your favorite nut butter.

MAKES 9

¾ cup (175g) unsalted butter, diced

3½oz (100g) dark (70%) chocolate, broken into small pieces

1½ cups (300g) sugar

½ tsp vanilla extract or paste

¾ cup plus 1 tbsp (100g) all-purpose flour

½ tsp baking powder

3 eggs

6 tbsp of your favorite nut butter (such as peanut butter or almond butter; use more or less according to taste)

1. Preheat the oven to 350°F (180°C).

2. Make the brownie batter, following steps 2–4 of the Original Chocolate Brownie recipe (see p12).

3. Pour the brownie batter into the prepared pan, spreading it evenly over the base. Add spoons of nut butter onto the brownie batter. Use a skewer to gently swirl the nut butter through the brownie batter to create a decorative marbled effect.

4. Bake for 35–40 minutes. It is done when the edges are set, and the center has risen and started to crack but may still look a bit soft and jiggly. Test with a toothpick (see step 6, p12).

5. Let cool completely in the pan on a wire rack for 1–2 hours. If you're in a hurry, pop the pan in the fridge for 30–45 minutes. Slice into 9 equal pieces and serve.

YOU WILL NEED

8 x 8 in (20 x 20 cm) square baking pan lined with parchment paper

Peanut Butter Salted Caramel Brownie

I've taken our classic chocolate brownie base and transformed it by creating a salted caramel layer running through the bake. I've included peanut butter and chopped, lightly salted peanuts for extra indulgence and texture, but if that isn't your bag, just leave them out.

MAKES 12

For the salted caramel

½ cup (100g) light brown sugar

¾ cup (175ml) heavy cream

4 tbsp (50g) unsalted butter, diced

1 tsp sea salt

1 cup (300g) crunchy peanut butter (optional)

For the brownie batter

¾ cup (175g) unsalted butter, diced

3½oz (100g) dark (70%) chocolate, broken into small pieces

1½ cups (300g) sugar

½ tsp vanilla extract or paste

¾ cup plus 1 tbsp (100g) all-purpose flour

½ tsp baking powder

3 eggs

½ cup (50g) lightly salted peanuts, chopped (optional)

1. Begin with the salted caramel. Combine the light brown sugar, heavy cream, butter, and sea salt in a saucepan set over low heat and stir until the sugar has dissolved.

2. Turn the heat up to medium and bubble the sauce for 2–3 minutes until it becomes golden and syrupy, being careful not to burn the sugar. Take off the heat and let cool slightly. Add the peanut butter, mix thoroughly, then spread the mixture evenly over the base of one prepared pan, right into the corners. Transfer the pan to the freezer while you prepare the brownie base. It will need about 1 hour to freeze completely.

3. Preheat the oven to 350°F (180C).

4. Make the brownie batter, following steps 2–4 of the Original Chocolate Brownie recipe (see p12).

5. To assemble and bake, pour half the brownie batter into the second prepared pan, spreading it evenly over the base.

6. Take the frozen salted caramel mixture from the freezer, remove it from the pan and carefully place it on top of the brownie batter in the pan. Pour the remaining brownie batter over the top, ensuring the caramel layer is completely covered and smoothing the top. Sprinkle over the chopped peanuts if using.

7. Bake for 40 minutes. It is done when the edges are set, and the center has risen and started to crack but may still look a bit soft and jiggly. Test with a toothpick (see step 6, p12).

8. Let cool completely in the pan on a wire rack for 1–2 hours. If you're in a hurry, pop the pan in the fridge for 30–45 minutes. Cut into 6 equal strips, then halve to make 12 bars, and serve.

pictured overleaf >>

YOU WILL NEED

Two 8 x 8 in (20 x 20 cm) square baking pans lined with parchment paper

Chili Chocolate Brownie

The idea for this one was to give the brownie a hint of spice—balancing the chili heat by combining it with cinnamon, rather than the fiery kind of heat that leaves you reaching for a cooling glass of milk. Feel free to spice it up with extra chili powder if you want more of a kick.

MAKES 9

¾ cup (175g) unsalted butter, diced

1 tsp chili powder

1 tsp ground cinnamon

3½oz (100g) dark (70%) chocolate, broken into small pieces

1½ cups (300g) sugar

½ tsp vanilla extract or paste

¾ cup plus 1 tbsp (100g) all-purpose flour

½ tsp baking powder

3 eggs

1. Preheat the oven to 350ºF (180C).

2. Make the brownie batter, following steps 2–4 of the Original Chocolate Brownie recipe on (see p12). At step 2, add the chili powder and cinnamon while the butter is melting to infuse the flavors.

3. Pour the batter into the prepared pan, spreading it evenly over the base, and bake for 30 minutes. It is done when the edges are set, and the center has risen and started to crack but may still look a bit soft and jiggly. Test with a toothpick (see step 6, p12).

4. Let cool completely in the pan on a wire rack for 1–2 hours. If you're in a hurry, pop the pan in the fridge for 30–45 minutes. Slice into 9 equal pieces and serve.

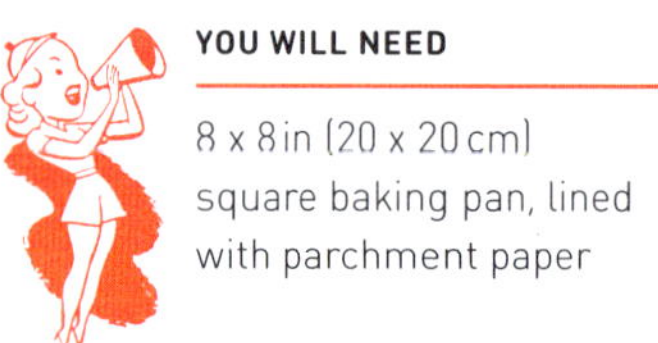

YOU WILL NEED

8 x 8 in (20 x 20 cm) square baking pan, lined with parchment paper

Ginger Drizzle Brownie

The simple but tasty addition of ginger pieces in a sugary syrup transforms our classic brownie base into something a bit more special—a warming treat of a dessert with a zesty ginger drizzle topping.

MAKES 9

¾ cup (175g) unsalted butter, diced

1 large piece preserved ginger, finely chopped

3½oz (100g) dark (70%) chocolate, broken into small pieces

1½ cups (300g) sugar

½ tsp vanilla extract or paste

¾ cup plus 1 tbsp (100g) all-purpose flour

½ tsp baking powder

1 tsp ground ginger

3 eggs

For the ginger drizzle topping

⅓ cup plus 1 tsp (70g) sugar

2 whole pieces from jar of preserved ginger, chopped into small pieces

2 tbsp ginger syrup from jar

1. Preheat the oven to 350°F (180°C).

2. Make the brownie batter, following steps 2–4 of the Original Chocolate Brownie recipe (see p12). Add the chopped preserved ginger while the butter is melting to help infuse the flavor throughout the brownies.

3. Pour the batter into the prepared pan, spreading it evenly over the base. Bake for 30–35 minutes. It is done when the edges are set, and the center has risen and started to crack but may still look a bit soft and jiggly. Test with a toothpick (see step 6, p12). Let cool in the pan on a wire rack for 1–2 hours.

4. Meanwhile, make the ginger drizzle topping. In a small bowl, mix the sugar, preserved ginger, ginger syrup, and 2 tablespoons water until the sugar has dissolved and the mixture has developed a syrupy consistency.

5. While the brownie is still a little warm, spoon the ginger drizzle topping over the surface. If you have a toothpick or a fine skewer, poke some small holes right through the brownie to allow the drizzle to reach the center more easily.

6. Let cool completely in the pan on a wire rack for 1–2 hours. If you're in a hurry, pop the pan in the fridge for 30–45 minutes. Slice into 9 equal pieces and serve.

YOU WILL NEED

8 x 8 in (20 x 20 cm) square baking pan lined with parchment paper

Bitter Orange Marmalade Brownie

Our chocolate orange brownies have been so popular over the years that I've played around with the flavors to create a subtle tangy twist that takes these brownies to another level.

MAKES 9

¾ cup (175g) unsalted butter, diced

1 tsp orange extract

1 tbsp orange marmalade

3½oz (100g) dark (70%) chocolate, broken into small pieces

1½ cups (300g) sugar

½ tsp vanilla extract or paste

¾ cup plus 1 tbsp (100g) all-purpose flour

½ tsp baking powder

3 eggs

For the bitter orange marmalade swirl

4½oz (125g) white chocolate

2 tbsp orange marmalade

⅓ cup (75ml) sour cream

1 egg, beaten

1 tsp orange food coloring

1. Preheat the oven to 350°F (180°C).

2. Make the brownie batter, following steps 2–4 of the Original Chocolate Brownie recipe (see p12). Add the orange extract and orange marmalade to the butter as it melts to infuse these flavors throughout the brownies.

3. For the marmalade swirl, put the white chocolate in a heatproof, microwave-safe bowl, cover, and carefully melt in short 10-second blasts on high power, stirring each time until the chocolate is smooth and melted (be very careful not to overheat).

4. Put the marmalade in a separate microwave-safe bowl and warm it gently for 10–15 seconds in the microwave to loosen the texture.

5. Mix the sour cream into the melted white chocolate. Mix in the egg, the warmed orange marmalade, and the orange food coloring until you have a smooth, evenly colored marmalade swirl mixture. Set aside.

6. Pour half of the brownie batter into the prepared baking pan. Carefully spoon over half of the marmalade swirl mixture onto this first layer of brownie batter. Pour the remaining brownie mixture over the swirl layer.

7. Dollop spoonfuls of the remaining marmalade swirl mixture on top of the brownie mix. Use a toothpick to make decorative swirl patterns in the top layer of batter.

8. Bake for 30–35 minutes. It is done when the edges are set, and the center has risen and started to crack but may still look a bit soft and jiggly. Test with a toothpick (see step 6, p12).

9. Let cool completely in the pan on a wire rack for 1–2 hours. If you're in a hurry, pop the pan in the fridge for 30–45 minutes. Slice into 9 equal pieces and serve.

YOU WILL NEED

8 x 8 in (20 x 20 cm) square baking pan lined with parchment paper

Espresso Martini Brownie

Anyone for a brownie cocktail? It's a yes from me. The coffee icing looks and tastes similar to the crema on the top of an espresso. These make the most perfect dessert for a party.

MAKES 9 BROWNIES OR 36 SMALL BITES

For the butter infusion

1 tsp juniper berries

1 tsp coriander seeds

6 cardamom pods

1 strip lemon peel

¾ cup (175g) unsalted
  butter, diced

For the brownie

3½oz (100g) dark (70%)
  chocolate, in small pieces

1½ cups (300g) sugar

½ tsp vanilla extract or paste

¾ cup plus 1 tbsp (100g)
  all-purpose flour

½ tsp baking powder

3 eggs

1½ tbsp gin (optional)

coffee beans, to decorate

For the buttercream icing

10 tbsp (150g) unsalted butter,
  softened

2½ cups (300g) powdered sugar

3 tbsp gin

2 tbsp instant coffee powder,
  plus extra to decorate (optional)

YOU WILL NEED

8 x 8in (20 x 20cm)
square baking pan lined
with parchment paper
8 x 8in (20 x 20cm) piece
cheesecloth

1. Preheat the oven to 350°F (180° C).

2. Begin by making the butter infusion. Wrap the juniper berries, coriander seeds, cardamom pods, and lemon peel in a piece of cheesecloth and tie with kitchen string to enclose. Melt the butter in a small pan over low heat, then add the bag. Maintain a very low simmer for 15–20 minutes to gently infuse the spices into the butter. Don't let the butter brown or burn. At the end of the cooking time, squeeze the bag gently to remove as much butter and flavoring as possible, then discard the bag and spices. This infused butter will be used for the brownie batter.

3. Add the chocolate pieces to the pan, and melt the chocolate into the infused butter. Follow steps 2–4 of the Original Chocolate Brownie recipe (see p12) to make the brownie batter.

4. Pour the brownie batter into the prepared pan, spreading it evenly over the base and bake for 30 minutes. It is done when the edges are set, and the center has risen and started to crack but may still look a bit soft and jiggly. Test with a toothpick (see step 6, p12). Let cool in the pan on a wire rack for 1–2 hours.

5. Meanwhile, for the buttercream icing, in a separate medium bowl, use a spatula to beat the butter for 1–2 minutes until light and fluffy. Sift in the powdered sugar and carefully mix until fully incorporated and smooth. Add the 3 tablespoons gin and the coffee powder and mix again until you have a smooth, well-combined icing.

6. Once it has cooled, prick the top of the brownie all over with a toothpick and drizzle over the 1½ tablespoons of gin, if using. Using a palette knife, spread the buttercream icing evenly over the top of the brownie. Decorate with a few coffee beans, and a sprinkling of coffee powder, if you like. Slice into 9 equal pieces and serve. For dessert bites, cut each brownie into 4 pieces for 36 bite-sized brownies.

pictured overleaf >>

Rum and Raisin Brownie

Raisins add an extra rich, chewy gooeyness, and rum gives a lovely warmth. Be warned—the spiced frosting is so ridiculously delicious that you may want to make extra. You will need to start this recipe the night before you plan to bake it.

MAKES 9 BROWNIES OR 36 SMALL BITES

For the rum and raisin infusion

½ cup (100g) raisins

5 tbsp rum

For the brownie

¾ cup (175g) unsalted butter, diced

3½oz (100g) dark (70%) chocolate, in small pieces

1½ cups (300g) sugar

½ tsp vanilla extract or paste

¾ cup plus 1 tbsp (100g) all-purpose flour

½ tsp baking powder

3 eggs

1½ tbsp rum, for drizzling

For the buttercream icing

10 tbsp (150g) unsalted butter, softened

2 cups plus 2 tbsp (300g) powdered sugar

2 tbsp raisins, chopped

3 tbsp rum

½ tsp ground allspice

1. For the rum and raisin infusion, put the raisins in a small bowl, pour over the rum, cover and set aside overnight to let the flavors infuse.

2. The next day, preheat the oven to 350°F (180°C).

3. Make the brownie batter, following steps 2–4 of the Original Chocolate Brownie recipe (see p12).

4. Gently mix in the infused raisins and rum and pour the batter into the prepared pan, spreading it evenly over the base. Bake for 30 minutes. It is done when the edges are set, and the center has risen and started to crack but may still look a bit soft and jiggly. Test with a toothpick (see step 6, p12). Let cool in the pan on a wire rack for 1–2 hours.

5. Meanwhile, for the buttercream icing, in a medium bowl, use a spatula to beat the butter for 1–2 minutes, until light and fluffy. Sift in the powdered sugar and carefully mix until fully incorporated and smooth. Add the chopped raisins, rum, and allspice and mix again until you have a smooth, well-combined icing.

6. Once the brownie has cooled, prick the top all over with a toothpick. Drizzle over the 1½ tablespoons rum, if using, for extra flavor. Using a palette knife, spread the buttercream icing evenly over the top of the brownie.

7. Slice into 9 equal pieces and serve. For dessert bites, cut each brownie piece into 4 to make 36 small, bite-sized brownies.

YOU WILL NEED

8 x 8in (20 x 20cm) square baking pan lined with parchment paper

Rhubarb Crumble and Custard Brownie

My take on that classic comfort food dessert, made by sandwiching sharp rhubarb compote and sour cream custard between layers of our classic brownie, and giving the whole thing a lovely, crunchy, shortbread topping.

MAKES 9

For the rhubarb compote

14oz (400g) fresh rhubarb plus 3¼ tbsp sugar or 19oz (540g) can rhubarb in light syrup

For the custard swirl

4½oz (125g) white chocolate, broken into small pieces

⅓ cup (75ml) sour cream

¼ tsp red food coloring (to give a pale pink rhubarb color)

2 tbsp vanilla extract or paste

1 egg, beaten

1. For the rhubarb compote, put the fresh rhubarb, sugar, and a splash of water, or canned rhubarb and its syrup, in a small pan over low heat. Cook, stirring to make sure the compote doesn't burn, until most of the liquid has evaporated. You will have a thick compote that will take 20–30 minutes. Set aside.

2. For the custard swirl, put the chocolate in a microwave-proof bowl, cover, and microwave in short, 10-second blasts on high power until it is completely melted, stirring as needed until the consistency is smooth (be very careful not to overheat).

3. Stir in the sour cream, red food coloring, and vanilla and mix well. Finally, stir in the egg until fully combined. Set aside.

4. To make the rhubarb compote and custard swirl layer, pour the rhubarb compote into one of the prepared baking pans. Using a spatula, spread half of the prepared custard swirl mixture over the rhubarb layer. Put the pan into the freezer and freeze until solid, about 1 hour.

5. Preheat the oven to 350°F (180°C).

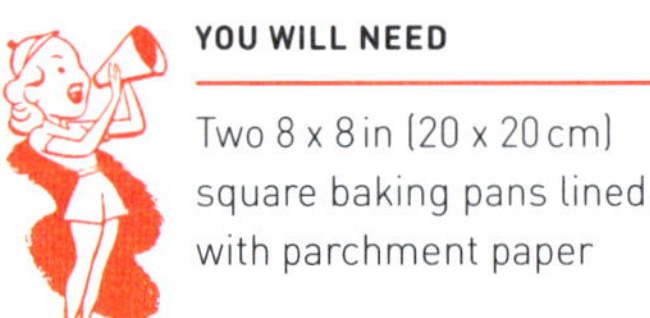

YOU WILL NEED

Two 8 x 8 in (20 x 20 cm) square baking pans lined with parchment paper

TIP

You can also change up this recipe by using any other fruit that gives a tart kick, such as Granny Smith apples, gooseberries, or even cranberries, which would make an excellent festive option.

For the brownie batter

¾ cup (175g) unsalted
  butter, diced

3½oz (100g) dark (70%)
  chocolate, broken into
  small pieces

1½ cups (300g) sugar

½ tsp vanilla extract or paste

¾ cup plus 1 tbsp (100g)
  all-purpose flour

½ tsp baking powder

3 eggs

For the topping

3 all-butter shortbread cookies

To serve

custard (optional)

6. Meanwhile, make the brownie batter, following steps 2–4 of the Original Chocolate Brownie recipe (see p12).

7. When the rhubarb compote and custard swirl layer has frozen solid, pour half of the brownie batter into the second prepared baking pan, spreading it evenly over the base. Carefully remove the frozen rhubarb layer from its pan and place it on top of the brownie batter. Spoon over the other half of brownie batter, smoothing it over the top.

8. Spoon the remaining custard swirl mixture over the top of the brownie mix and use a toothpick to swirl it through.

9. For the topping, break the shortbread cookies into a mix of larger pieces and light crumbs. Sprinkle over the top of the brownie, then bake for 45 minutes. It is done when the edges are set, and the center has risen and started to crack but may still look a bit soft and jiggly. Test with a toothpick (see step 6, p12).

10. Let cool completely in the pan on a wire rack for 1–2 hours. If you are in a hurry, pop the pan in the fridge for 30–45 minutes. Slice into 9 equal pieces and serve dolloped with custard, if you like.

pictured overleaf >>

Raspberry Ripple Brownie

Childhood memories of summers spent at the seaside was my inspiration for this recipe. Regardless of the weather, I had to have a Whippy ice cream. Add some raspberry topping, and it became a taste sensation, never forgotten.

MAKES 9

¾ cup (175g) unsalted butter, diced

3½oz (100g) dark (70%) chocolate, broken into small pieces

1½ cups (300g) sugar

½ tsp vanilla extract or paste

¾ cup plus 1 tbsp (100g) all-purpose flour

½ tsp baking powder

3 eggs

For the raspberry swirl

4½oz (125g) white chocolate

⅓ cup (75ml) sour cream

1 egg, beaten

1 tsp natural raspberry flavoring

1 tbsp raspberry jam

1. Preheat the oven to 350°F (180°C).

2. Make the brownie batter, following steps 2–4 of the Original Chocolate Brownie recipe (see p12).

3. For the raspberry swirl, put the chocolate in a microwave-proof bowl, cover, and microwave in short 10-second blasts on high power, stirring each time until it is smooth and melted (be very careful not to overheat). Using a spatula, mix the sour cream into the melted white chocolate. Add the egg, raspberry flavoring, and raspberry jam, and mix until you have a smooth, well-combined raspberry swirl mixture.

4. Pour half of the brownie batter into the prepared baking pan, spreading it evenly over the base. Carefully spoon over half of the raspberry swirl mixture onto this first layer of brownie batter. Pour the remaining brownie batter over the swirl layer. Dollop spoonfuls of the remaining raspberry swirl mixture on top of the brownie batter. Use a toothpick to make decorative swirl patterns into the top layer of batter.

5. Bake for 35–40 minutes. It is done when the edges are set, and the center has risen and started to crack but may still look a bit soft and jiggly. Test with a toothpick (see step 6, p12).

6. Let cool completely in the pan on a wire rack for 1–2 hours. If you're in a hurry, pop the pan in the fridge for 30–45 minutes. Slice into 9 equal pieces and serve.

YOU WILL NEED

8 x 8 in (20 x 20 cm) square baking pan lined with parchment paper

Battenberg Brownie

This delicious and visually graphic treat, inspired by the classic Battenberg cake, is a brownie, a blondie, and marzipan, all presented in the signature checkerboard pattern.

MAKES 18

For the brownie batter

¾ cup (175g) unsalted
  butter, diced

3½oz (100g) dark (70%)
  chocolate, broken into
  small pieces

1½ cups (300g) sugar

½ tsp vanilla extract or paste

¾ cup plus 1 tbsp (100g)
  all-purpose flour

½ tsp baking powder

3 eggs

**For the pink almond
blondie batter**

¾ cup (175g) unsalted butter,
  diced

5½oz (150g) white chocolate,
  broken into small pieces

1½ cups (300g) sugar

½ tsp vanilla extract or paste

1 cup plus 2 tbsp (150g)
  all-purpose flour

½ tsp baking powder

3 eggs

½ tsp almond extract

½ tsp red food coloring

YOU WILL NEED

Two 8 x 8 in (20 x 20 cm)
square baking pans lined
with parchment paper

1. Preheat the oven to 350°F (180°C).

2. For the brownie batter, follow steps 2–4 of the Original Chocolate Brownie recipe (see p12). Pour the brownie batter into a prepared baking pan, spreading it evenly over the base. Set aside.

3. For the pink almond blondie batter, put a medium, heavy-based saucepan over medium heat. Add the butter and melt slowly, stirring continuously until the butter has melted (don't let it burn). Turn the heat to low, add the white chocolate and, using a spatula, keep stirring until the chocolate has melted completely into the butter and you have a smooth, glossy mixture.

4. Take the pan off the heat. Add the sugar and vanilla to the bowl and mix thoroughly. Add the flour and baking powder to the bowl and mix into the wet ingredients until you have a fine chocolatey mixture that resembles breadcrumbs, with no lumps of flour or sugar visible.

5. In a separate, medium bowl, whisk the eggs for 20–30 seconds until light and frothy. Add the almond extract and red food coloring to the whisked eggs and mix until the color is a uniform vibrant pink. Using a large metal spoon, carefully fold the colored eggs through the blondie mixture, trying to keep as much air in them as possible, to form a smooth batter. Pour the pink almond blondie batter into the second baking pan, spreading it evenly over the base.

6. Bake the brownie bases for 30–35 minutes and blondie bases for 35–40 minutes. They are done when the edges are set, and the center has risen and started to crack but may still look a bit soft and jiggly. Test with a toothpick (see step 6, p12). Let both bases cool in their pans on a wire rack for 1–2 hours before removing them from their pans.

recipe continues >>

To assemble

½ cup (125g) apricot jam,
  warmed to loosen

powdered sugar for dusting
  (optional)

three 16oz (454g) packages
  of ready-to-roll marzipan

7. Once completely cool, use a serrated knife to trim away the outer edges of both the chocolate brownie and pink almond blondie bases so they are neat and square.

8. Cut the brownies and the pink blondies into 6 strips of equal width, so you have 12 equal-sized strips in total (6 chocolate and 6 pink).

9. To assemble, start with two chocolate strips and two pink blondie strips for each Battenberg brownie block. Use a pastry brush to spread a thin layer of apricot jam over each strip of brownie/blondie, then assemble them into a 2 x 2 checkerboard square with alternating colors (chocolate-pink on the bottom row, pink-chocolate on the top row, or vice versa), pressing them gently together. Repeat twice more with the remaining brownie and blondie strips to make 3 Battenberg brownie blocks.

10. Lightly dust a work surface with powdered sugar or roll the marzipan between two pieces of plastic wrap to prevent sticking.

11. Roll out each pack of marzipan into a rectangle approximately 14 x 8 in (36 x 20 cm). You will need one rectangle per assembled Battenberg brownie block.

12. Using a pastry brush, spread a thin layer of apricot jam over the surface of each marzipan rectangle. Place one assembled Battenberg brownie block onto the center of the jam-coated marzipan rectangle. Roll the marzipan tightly around the brownie block, enclosing on four sides and leaving the ends exposed. Ensure there are no air pockets, and the seam is neatly tucked on the underside.

13. Trim the ends of the marzipan-wrapped brownies to neaten them and reveal the checkerboard pattern. Using a sharp knife, carefully slice your Battenbergs into individual squares (keeping the checkerboard pattern exposed). Cut each block into 6 pieces for 18 servings.

Strawberries and Cream Brownie

This creation takes our classic chocolate brownie base and infuses it with the sweet, fruity notes of strawberries. Top it off with a creamy strawberry swirl, and the result is a wonderfully moist and indulgent treat.

MAKES 9

¾ cup (175g) unsalted
  butter, diced

3½oz (100g) dark (70%)
  chocolate, broken into
  small pieces

1½ cups (300g) sugar

½ tsp vanilla extract or paste

¾ cup plus 1 tbsp (100g)
  all-purpose flour

½ tsp baking powder

3 eggs

For the strawberry swirl

4½oz (125g) white chocolate

⅓ cup (75ml) sour cream

1 egg, beaten

1 tbsp strawberry
  milkshake mix

1 tbsp strawberry jam

a few drops of red or pink food
  coloring (optional)

1. Make the brownie batter, following steps 2–4 of the Original Chocolate Brownie recipe (see p12).

2. For the strawberry swirl, put the white chocolate in a heatproof, microwave-safe bowl, cover, and carefully melt in short 10-second blasts on high power, stirring each time until the chocolate is smooth and melted (be very careful not to overheat).

3. Preheat the oven to 350°F (180°C).

4. Thoroughly mix the sour cream into the melted white chocolate, followed by the egg, strawberry milkshake mix, strawberry jam, and the food coloring (if using) until you have a smooth, evenly colored mixture.

5. To assemble, pour half of the brownie batter into the prepared pan, using a spatula to spread it evenly over the base. Carefully spoon over half of the strawberry swirl mixture onto this first layer of brownie batter, spreading it right to the edges. Pour the remaining brownie mixture over the swirl, spreading it to the edges.

6. Dollop spoonfuls of the remaining strawberry swirl mixture onto the top of the brownie mix. Use a toothpick to make decorative swirls in the top layer of batter.

7. Bake for 40–45 minutes. It is done when the edges are set and the center has risen and started to crack but may still look a bit soft and jiggly. Test with a toothpick (see step 6, p12).

8. Let cool completely in the pan on a wire rack for 1–2 hours. If you're in a hurry, pop the pan in the fridge for 30–45 minutes. Slice into 9 equal pieces and serve.

YOU WILL NEED

8 x 8 in (20 x 20 cm) square baking pan lined with parchment paper

Toffee Crisp Brownie

Chewy, crispy, fudgy... Simply put, this is my holy trio. We've used versions of this recipe for everything from kids' party cakes to grown-up snacking, and everything in between.

MAKES 12

For the chewy toffee crisp center

3 tbsp (50g) unsalted butter

½ cup (100g) brown sugar

3 tbsp corn syrup

1½ cups (40g) crispy rice cereal

For the brownie batter

¾ cup (175g) unsalted butter, diced

3½oz (100g) dark (70%) chocolate, broken into small pieces

1½ cups (300g) sugar

½ tsp vanilla extract or paste

¾ cup plus 1 tbsp (100g) all-purpose flour

½ tsp baking powder

3 eggs

For the chocolate topping

9oz (250g) milk chocolate

1. Start with the chewy toffee crisp center. In a saucepan, gently melt the butter, light brown sugar, and corn syrup over low heat. Stir continuously until all the ingredients are melted and thoroughly combined, forming a smooth caramel. Remove the saucepan from the heat and let the caramel cool slightly for a few minutes.

2. Working quickly so the caramel doesn't harden, stir in the crispy rice cereal until it is well coated in the caramel mixture. Be careful, as the caramel will be hot.

3. Using the back of a spoon, press this mixture evenly into a prepared baking pan, forming a flat layer. Put the pan into the freezer and freeze for 1 hour until the toffee crisp mixture is frozen solid. This step is crucial to create a distinct, firm layer that can be easily handled and inserted into brownie batter.

4. Preheat the oven to 350°F (180°C).

5. For the brownie base layer, make the batter, following steps 2–4 of the Original Chocolate Brownie recipe (see p12).

6. Pour half of the brownie batter into the second prepared pan, spreading it out evenly over the base. Carefully remove the frozen toffee crisp layer from the freezer and gently peel off the parchment paper.

7. Place the frozen toffee crisp layer directly on top of the first layer of brownie batter in the pan. Pour the remaining brownie batter over the frozen toffee crisp layer, ensuring it is completely covered, spreading the batter out to the edges.

8. Bake for 35–40 minutes. It is done when the edges are set, and the center has risen and started to crack but may still look a bit soft and jiggly. Test with a toothpick (see step 6, p12).

YOU WILL NEED

Two 8 x 8 in (20 cm) square baking pans lined with parchment paper

recipe continues >>

9. Let the brownie cool completely in the pan on a wire rack for 1–2 hours. Cooling completely is essential for the structure to set properly before adding the topping and slicing.

10. Once the brownie has cooled, melt the milk chocolate. Set a heatproof bowl over a saucepan of simmering water, making sure the bottom of the bowl does not touch the water in the pan beneath it. Break the chocolate into pieces and gently melt, stirring until the chocolate is smooth and glossy.

11. Carefully pour the melted chocolate evenly over the cooled brownie, using a spatula to spread it smoothly over the surface.

12. Put the pan in the refrigerator to let the chocolate layer set completely. This will take at least 1 hour.

13. Once fully set, carefully remove the brownie from the pan using the parchment paper to help you. Using a sharp knife, cut the chilled brownie into 6 even strips, then halve to make 12 bars.

TIPS

To maintain that wonderfully crisp texture, and to keep the chocolate firm, these brownies are best stored chilled.

For the ultimate texture, keep them in an airtight plastic container in the refrigerator.

Cookie Dough Brownie

One to feed the inner child in all of us, with a sweet, buttery, chocolate-chip topping. Pure perfection served warm with a big spoon of ice cream.

MAKES 9

¾ cup (175g) unsalted
  butter, diced

3½oz (100g) dark (70%)
  chocolate, broken into
  small pieces

1½ cups (300g) sugar

½ tsp vanilla extract or paste

¾ cup plus 1 tbsp (100g)
  all-purpose flour

½ tsp baking powder

3 eggs

For the cookie dough

5 tbsp (75g) unsalted
  butter, softened

3¼ tbsp (40g) light brown sugar

3¼ tbsp (40g) sugar

1 tsp vanilla extract or paste

1 egg

¾ cup plus 2 tbsp (115g)
  all-purpose flour

¼ tsp baking soda

pinch of salt

⅓ cup (50g) plain chocolate
  chips

1. Preheat the oven to 350°F (180°C).

2. To make the brownie batter, follow steps 2–4 of the Original Chocolate Brownie recipe (see p12).

3. For the cookie dough, put the butter and both types of sugar in a medium bowl and beat with a spatula for 1–2 minutes until creamy. Beat in the vanilla and egg. Sift the flour, baking soda, and pinch of salt into the bowl and mix it in with a wooden spoon. Stir in the chocolate chips.

4. Using a teaspoon, take small scoops of the cookie dough mixture, spacing them evenly and well apart, and dollop them onto the top of the brownie mixture in the pan. Bake for 35–40 minutes.

5. It is done when the edges are set, and the center has risen and started to crack but may still look a bit soft and jiggly. Some of the cookie dough will have sunk into the brownie, while any cookie dough on the surface will have turned a lovely golden brown. Test with a toothpick (see step 6, p12).

6. Let cool completely in the pan on a wire rack for 1–2 hours. If you're in a hurry, pop the pan in the fridge for 30–45 minutes. Slice into 9 equal pieces and serve.

pictured overleaf >>

YOU WILL NEED

8 x 8 in (20 x 20 cm)
square baking pan lined
with parchment paper

Pineapple and Coconut Upside-Down Brownie

Retro tropical loveliness, with sticky glazed pineapple rings and nutty dried coconut, all wrapped up in a decadent brownie batter. A super-rich treat.

MAKES 9

For the topping

6 tbsp (85g) unsalted butter

½ cup (100g) light or dark brown sugar

8oz (227g) can pineapple rings, drained, juice retained

4 candied cherries

For the brownie batter

¾ cup (175g) unsalted butter, diced

3½oz (100g) dark (70%) chocolate, broken into small pieces

1½ cups (300g) sugar

½ tsp vanilla extract or paste

¾ cup plus 1 tbsp (100g) all-purpose flour

½ tsp baking powder

3 eggs

⅔ cup (50g) shredded, unsweetened coconut

2 tbsp pineapple syrup (from the canned pineapple for the topping)

YOU WILL NEED

8 x 8 in (20 x 20 cm) square baking pan lined with parchment paper

1. Start with the topping. Combine the butter and sugar in a small saucepan over medium heat. Stir occasionally for 7–10 minutes, until the butter has melted and the sugar has dissolved to form a light caramel mixture. Take the caramel off the heat. Arrange the drained pineapple rings neatly in the prepared baking pan in a single layer, and place a candied cherry in the center of each ring. Pour the caramel over and around the pineapple, using a spatula to spread it to the edges.

2. Put the pan in the refrigerator to chill for a few minutes while you prepare the brownie batter; chilling will help the topping hold its shape when baked.

3. Preheat the oven to 350°F (180°C).

4. For the brownie batter, follow steps 2–4 of the Original Chocolate Brownie recipe (see p12). Fold the coconut and pineapple syrup into the batter.

5. Remove the prepared pan from the refrigerator. Carefully pour the brownie batter over the pineapple and caramel topping in the pan, spreading it evenly and being careful to keep the pineapple rings and cherries in place.

6. Bake for 40–45 minutes. It is done when the edges are set, and the center has risen and started to crack but may still look a bit soft and jiggly. Test with a toothpick (see step 6, p12).

7. Remove the brownie from the oven and let cool in the pan on a wire rack for 15 minutes. Carefully invert the slightly cooled brownie onto a cake stand or serving plate.

8. For the cleanest slices, it is best to cool the brownie completely at room temperature before slicing into 9 equal serving pieces.

Sticky Toffee Brownie

Our classic chocolate brownie base is infused with the rich, caramelized flavors of sticky toffee pudding. The result? A wonderfully moist and indulgent treat, drenched in a luscious toffee sauce. I recommend using Medjool dates for their deep caramel notes.

MAKES 9

8oz (225g) pitted Medjool
dates, chopped

1 tsp baking soda

¾ cup (175g) unsalted
butter, diced

3½oz (100g) dark (70%) chocolate,
broken into small pieces

1½ cups (300g) dark brown sugar

½ tsp vanilla extract or paste

1 tbsp molasses

¾ cup plus 1 tbsp (100g)
all-purpose flour

½ tsp baking powder

½ cup (50g) chopped
walnuts (optional)

3 eggs

1. Put the dates in a heatproof bowl with the baking soda and ⅔ cup (150ml) boiling water. Let sit for 10 minutes to soften the dates. The mixture may bubble up, which is normal.

2. Once the dates are softened, drain them, then puree the dates using an immersion blender or food processor. If needed, use some of the soaking liquid to loosen the dates while blending. The mixture should have the consistency of a thick, sticky jam. Set aside.

3. To make the brownie batter, follow step 2 of the Original Chocolate Brownie recipe (see p12).

4. Take the pan off the heat. Add the sugar, vanilla, and the 1 tablespoon molasses to the pan and mix thoroughly. Add the flour and baking powder and mix into the wet ingredients until you have a fine, chocolatey mixture that resembles breadcrumbs, with no lumps of flour or sugar visible. Stir in the chopped walnuts, if using.

5. Preheat the oven to 350°F (180°C).

6. In a medium bowl, whisk the eggs for 20–30 seconds until light and frothy. Using a large metal spoon, carefully fold the whisked eggs through the brownie mixture, keeping as much air in the mixture as possible, to form a smooth batter. Fold the prepared date puree through the brownie batter until fully incorporated. The batter will be quite runny at this stage.

7. Pour the batter in the prepared baking pan, spreading it evenly over the base. Bake for 35–40 minutes. It is done when the edges are set and the center has risen and started to crack but may still look a bit soft and jiggly. Test with a toothpick (see step 6, p12).

recipe continues >>

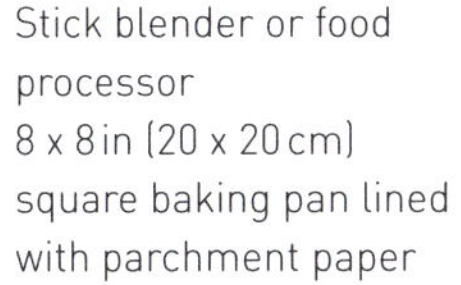

YOU WILL NEED

Stick blender or food
processor
8 x 8in (20 x 20cm)
square baking pan lined
with parchment paper

For the sticky toffee sauce

6 tbsp (100g) unsalted butter

⅓ cup (70g) dark brown sugar

½ cup (120ml) heavy cream

1 tsp molasses

8. Meanwhile, make the sticky toffee sauce. In a small saucepan, melt the butter over low-medium heat. Whisk in the sugar and continue whisking until the sugar has dissolved and the sauce is smooth. This should take 3–5 minutes.

9. Slowly pour in the heavy cream, whisking gently to combine. Once the mixture is hot (do not let it boil), stir in the 1 teaspoon black molasses until melted and well combined. Remove from the heat. The sauce will thicken as it cools.

10. To serve as a hot pudding, pour the warm sticky toffee sauce generously over the still-warm brownie base. Prick the top of the brownie all over with a toothpick to help the sauce to soak into the brownie. Slice into 9 equal pieces and serve with ice cream.

11. For a warm dessert with a firmer texture, let the cooked brownie cool completely in the pan on a wire rack for 1–2 hours, before making and adding the sauce. Pour the warm, sticky toffee sauce generously over the cooled brownie base. Prick the top of the brownie all over with a toothpick to help the sauce to soak into the brownie. Slice into 9 equal pieces and serve.

Orange and Almond Brownie

Bright citrus from cooked, pureed oranges and the nuttiness of ground almonds transform the classic chocolate brownie to give it a moist, yielding texture.

MAKES 9

2 unwaxed oranges, scrubbed

¾ cup (175g) unsalted butter, diced

3½oz (100g) dark (70%) chocolate, broken into small pieces

1½ cups (300g) sugar

½ tsp vanilla extract or paste

1¼ cups (150g) all-purpose flour

½ tsp baking powder

½ cup (50g) ground almonds

3 eggs

For the topping

1oz (25g) white chocolate

a few drops of orange food coloring

sliced almonds

YOU WILL NEED

Food processor
8 x 8 in (20 x 20 cm) square baking pan lined with parchment paper

1. Put the oranges in a saucepan with a lid and cover with water. Bring to a boil, then reduce the heat, cover with the lid, and simmer gently for about 1½ hours, or until the oranges are very soft when pierced with a fork. Check the water levels and add more water as needed to keep the fruit covered. Drain the oranges and let them cool completely.

2. Once cool enough to handle, cut the oranges open, remove and discard any pips, then puree the oranges, including the peels, in a food processor until completely smooth. Set aside.

3. Preheat the oven to 350°F (180°C).

4. To make the brownie batter, follow step 2 of the Original Chocolate Brownie recipe (see p12). Take the pan off the heat. Add the sugar and vanilla to the pan and mix thoroughly. Stir in the pureed oranges until well combined.

5. In a large bowl, combine the flour, baking powder, and ground almonds, mixing well. Add these dry ingredients to the mixture in the pan and combine thoroughly.

6. In another bowl, whisk the eggs for 20–30 seconds, until light and frothy. Using a large metal spoon, carefully fold the whisked eggs through the chocolate and orange mixture, keeping as much air in the mixture as possible, to form a smooth batter. Pour the batter into the prepared pan, spreading it evenly over the base.

7. Bake for 35 minutes. It is done when the edges are set and the center has risen and started to crack but may still look a bit soft and jiggly. Test with a toothpick (see step 6, p12). Let cool completely in the pan on a wire rack for 1–2 hours.

8. Meanwhile, for the topping, put the white chocolate and food coloring in a heatproof, microwave-safe bowl, cover, and carefully melt in short 10-second blasts on high power, stirring each time until the chocolate is smooth, melted, and evenly colored (be very careful not to let it overheat).

9. Drizzle the topping over the brownie to decorate, and sprinkle over the sliced almonds. Slice into 9 equal pieces and serve.

Burnt Basque Cheesecake Brownie

The "burnt" Basque cheesecake has gained cult status for its dramatic look and caramel taste. Our brownie version combines the best of both worlds—a classic chocolate brownie base with a distinctively creamy and bittersweet Basque cheesecake topping. This recipe has it all.

SERVES 9–12

¾ cup (175g) unsalted butter, diced, plus extra for greasing

3½oz (100g) dark (70%) chocolate, broken into small pieces

1½ cups (300g) sugar

½ tsp vanilla extract or paste

¾ cup plus 1 tbsp (100g) all-purpose flour

½ tsp baking powder

3 eggs

YOU WILL NEED

8in (20cm) round, loose-bottomed or springform cake pan, at least 2in (5cm) deep
Hand-held mixer or blender

1. Butter the loose-bottomed or springform cake pan. Lay out two large sheets of parchment paper, one on top of the other, with one sheet turned 90 degrees so the corners point in opposite directions.

2. Push the parchment paper into the cake pan, pressing into the edges and making sure plenty of paper is sticking out at least 2in (5cm) above the rim. Press the creases up the sides, but don't worry about lining the pan too neatly—the grooves in the parchment give this cheesecake its characteristic look.

3. For the brownie, make the batter, following steps 2–4 of the Original Chocolate Brownie recipe (see p12).

4. Pour the brownie batter into the prepared cake pan, spreading it evenly over the base. Set aside.

5. Make the topping in a large mixing bowl using an immersion blender, or in the bowl of a mixer. Put the cream cheese and sugar in the bowl and beat for 1–2 minutes, until the sugar has dissolved—check this by rubbing a little of the mixture between your fingertips. If it still feels grainy, keep mixing for another minute or so.

6. Add the flour, sour cream, eggs, vanilla, and salt to the bowl and mix again until the mixture has a smooth consistency.

7. Preheat the oven to 350°F (180°C) for the initial bake. Ensure there is plenty of oven space above the middle shelf.

8. Carefully pour the Basque cheesecake mixture over the brownie batter in the cake pan, using a spatula to scrape out every last bit. Give the pan a sharp bang on the countertop to remove any air bubbles. Bake for 50 minutes.

**For the burnt Basque
cheesecake topping**

1¾ cups (400g) full-fat
   cream cheese

½ cup plus 1 tbsp (115g) sugar

1 tbsp all-purpose flour

½ cup (100ml) sour cream

2 eggs, beaten

1 tsp vanilla extract or paste

pinch of salt

9. After 50 minutes, increase the oven temperature to 425°F (220°C) and bake for a further 20 minutes. When it's cooked, it should have a deeply caramelized top and be puffed up like a soufflé. The cheesecake layer will still have a wobble when you shake the pan.

10. Let the cheesecake brownie cool completely in the pan for 1–2 hours. The cheesecake layer will sink as it cools, creating its characteristic craterlike shape. Once cooled, chill in the refrigerator for at least 1 hour before releasing the collar of the pan. For a more intense flavor and creamy texture, chill for at least 2 hours or even overnight.

11. To cut clean slices, use a large, sharp knife and wipe the blade using paper towel between each slice.

pictured overleaf >>

TIP

*Please note that while
the initial baking
temperature is the
same as for our original
brownie, the final,
higher temperature will
give you the signature
"burnt" top that's
characteristic of the
classic Basque
cheesecake.*

Honey Toffee and Almond Brownie

Homemade toffee brittle takes a bit of patience but is so worth it! The result is a rich, chocolatey brownie with crunchy, nutty, caramel notes in every bite.

MAKES 9

For the honey toffee brittle

½ cup plus 2 tbsp (120g) sugar

3 tbsp (40g) unsalted butter

2 tbsp honey

1 cup (100g) hazelnuts, finely chopped

1 tbsp all-purpose flour

1. Preheat the oven to 350°F (180°C).

2. Begin with the honey toffee brittle. In a saucepan over medium heat, combine the sugar and butter, stirring in 2 tablespoons of water. When the mixture boils, turn the heat down to low and stir in the honey.

3. Cook the mixture, stirring regularly, until it caramelizes to form a toffee, and reaches the hard crack stage (295–310°F/ 146–155°C when tested on a sugar thermometer). At this point, a small amount of the liquid dropped into a glass of cold water will harden instantly into brittle threads that break with a clean snap. It will take 20–30 minutes for the toffee to reach this stage, so be patient. When it's ready, set aside to cool for 2–3 minutes.

4. Spread the hazelnuts evenly over the small, parchment paper–lined baking pan then lightly toast in the oven for 10 minutes. Set aside to cool slightly. Keep the oven on.

5. Once the toffee has cooled slightly but is still liquid, pour it evenly over the toasted nuts on the parchment paper to make a brittle. Allow this brittle to cool completely and harden, about 1 hour, then break into small, irregular pieces. Dust three-quarters of the brittle pieces in the flour. This will prevent the brittle pieces from sinking to the bottom of the brownie when baking. Set aside the remaining one-quarter of the pieces for decoration.

YOU WILL NEED

Sugar thermometer
Small baking pan lined with parchment paper
8 x 8 in (20 x 20 cm) square baking pan lined with parchment paper

For the brownie

¾ cup (175g) unsalted
  butter, diced

3½oz (100g) dark (70%)
  chocolate, broken into
  small pieces

1½ cups (300g) sugar

½ tsp vanilla extract or paste

¾ cup plus 1 tbsp (100g)
  all-purpose flour

½ tsp baking powder

3 eggs

6. For the brownie, make the batter, following steps 2–4 of the Original
   Chocolate Brownie recipe (see p12).

7. Gently fold the flour-dusted toffee brittle pieces into the brownie
   batter until just distributed. Pour the batter into the prepared
   square baking pan, spreading it evenly over the base.

8. Bake for 35–40 minutes. It is done when the edges are set, and
   the center has risen and started to crack but may still look a bit
   soft and jiggly. Test with a toothpick (see step 6, p12).

9. While the brownie is still warm, sprinkle the reserved toffee
   brittle pieces over the top for decoration. Let cool completely
   in the pan on a wire rack for 1–2 hours before slicing into
   9 equal serving pieces.

Key Lime Pie Brownie

A fabulous brownie created by combining the rich chocolate original with bright key lime flavors and a crisp base, all topped with fluffy whipped cream.

MAKES 9

For the graham cracker base

7oz (200g) graham crackers

5 tbsp (75g) unsalted
  butter, melted

For the brownie batter

¾ cup (175g) unsalted
  butter, diced

juice and finely grated zest of
  1 unwaxed lime

5½oz (150g) dark (70%)
  chocolate, broken into
  small pieces

1½ cups (300g) sugar

½ tsp vanilla extract or paste

1¼ cups (150g) all-purpose flour

½ tsp baking powder

3 eggs

1. Start with the graham cracker base. Crush the graham crackers into fine crumbs using a food processor or by placing them in a sealed bag and crushing with a rolling pin.

2. Combine the graham cracker crumbs and melted butter in a bowl, mixing until the crumbs are evenly coated. Press this mixture firmly and evenly into the base of the prepared baking pan, using the back of a spoon to compact it evenly. Let cool.

3. For the brownie, make the batter, following steps 2–4 of the Original Chocolate Brownie recipe (see p12). Add the lime zest to the butter as it melts to help infuse the flavor throughout the brownie. When you have folded the whisked eggs into the batter, stir in the lime juice until just combined.

4. Pour the brownie batter over the cooled graham cracker base in the pan, spreading it evenly over the graham cracker layer. Put the pan in the refrigerator for 1 hour to let the mixture cool and slightly set.

recipe continues >>

YOU WILL NEED

Food processor (optional)
8 x 8 in (20 x 20 cm)
square baking pan lined
with parchment paper
Electric hand whisk
Piping bag fitted with a
star nozzle (optional)

For the key lime filling and whipped cream topping

4 large egg yolks

14oz (397g) can sweetened
  condensed milk

juice and finely grated zest of
  4 unwaxed limes (about ½ cup
  or 120ml)

⅔ cup (150ml) heavy cream

extra lime zest (or lime slices),
  to garnish

5. Meanwhile, prepare the key lime filling. In a large mixing bowl, use an electric hand whisk to whisk the egg yolks, sweetened condensed milk, and the lime juice and zest until well combined and smooth. The mixture will thicken slightly as it sits.

6. Preheat the oven to 350°F (180°C). To assemble the brownie, pour the key lime filling mixture evenly over the cooled and slightly set brownie layer in the baking pan. Bake for 55–60 minutes, or until the center is mostly set but still slightly jiggly when gently shaken. Test with a toothpick (see step 6, p12).

7. Set aside to cool completely on a wire rack for at least 2 hours, or until the bottom of the pan is cool to the touch. This is crucial for the filling to set properly. Once cooled, remove the brownie from the pan.

8. Just before serving, use an electric hand whisk to whisk the cream until firm. Decorate as you like. It could be as simple as just spreading the cream over the top using a palette knife and sprinkling with extra lime zest. Or go full-out, making a decorative pattern using a piping bag fitted with a star nozzle and garnishing with extra lime zest or lime slices.

9. To cut clean slices, dip a sharp knife into hot water before each cut, wiping the knife clean and dipping it into hot water again before cutting again. Leftovers can be stored in the fridge, loosely covered, for 3–4 days.

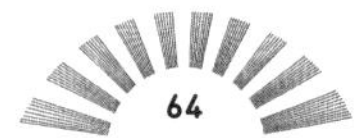

Pear and Hazelnut Brownie

Sometimes, the simplest things are the best. Few flavor combinations could be as delightful as a chocolate brownie topped with sliced pears and chopped hazelnuts.

MAKES 9

¾ cup (175g) unsalted butter, diced

3½oz (100g) dark (70%) chocolate, broken into small pieces

1½ cups (300g) sugar

½ tsp vanilla extract or paste

¾ cup plus 1 tbsp (100g) all-purpose flour

½ tsp baking powder

3 eggs

2 ripe but firm pears, unpeeled, cored and thinly sliced

⅓ cup (50g) chopped hazelnuts

1. Preheat the oven to 350°F (180°C).

2. For the brownie, make the batter, following steps 2–4 of the Original Chocolate Brownie recipe (see p12).

3. Pour the batter into a prepared baking pan, then arrange the sliced pears evenly over the top of the brownie batter. Sprinkle the chopped hazelnuts over the top.

4. Bake for 30–35 minutes. It is done when the edges are set, and the center has risen and started to crack but may still look a bit soft and jiggly. Test with a toothpick (see step 6, p12).

5. Let cool in the pan on a wire rack, for 1–2 hours, then slice into 9 equal serving pieces.

YOU WILL NEED

8 x 8 in (20 x 20 cm) square baking pan lined with parchment paper

St. Patrick's Day Brownie

Featuring a rich stout-infused brownie base, a smooth Irish cream buttercream icing, and festive green and orange chocolate decoration.

MAKES 36 SMALL BITES

15fl oz (440ml) can stout beer

¾ cup (175g) unsalted butter, diced

3½oz (100g) dark (70%) chocolate, broken into small pieces

1½ cups (300g) sugar

½ tsp vanilla extract or paste

¾ cup plus 1 tbsp (100g) all-purpose flour

½ tsp baking powder

3 eggs

For the Irish cream buttercream icing and decoration

5 tbsp (75g) unsalted butter, softened

1¼ cups (150g) powdered sugar

1 tsp vanilla extract or paste

2–3 tablespoons Irish cream

1¾oz (50g) white chocolate

green and orange food coloring (gel or liquid)

YOU WILL NEED

8 x 8in (20 x 20cm) square baking pan lined with parchment paper

1. Pour the beer into a small saucepan. Bring to a simmer over medium heat then reduce until about ½ cup (125ml) of liquid remains, 20–30 minutes. Stir occasionally to prevent sticking. Remove from heat and allow the reduction to cool completely. This is crucial for the liquid to be incorporated properly into the brownie batter.

2. Preheat the oven to 350°F (180°C).

3. For the brownie, make the batter, following steps 2–4 of the Original Chocolate Brownie recipe (see p12). Fold the cooled stout-beer reduction into the batter until just combined.

4. Pour the batter into the prepared pan, spreading it evenly over the base, and bake for 30–35 minutes. It is done when the edges are set, and the center has risen and started to crack but may still look a bit soft and jiggly. Test with a toothpick (see step 6, p12). Let cool completely in the pan on a wire rack for 1–2 hours before adding the icing.

5. For the Irish cream buttercream icing, in a bowl use a spatula to beat the butter for 2–3 minutes until light and fluffy. Sift in the powdered sugar and carefully mix until fully incorporated and smooth. Add the vanilla and Irish cream and mix until smooth. Start with 2 tablespoons of liqueur and add more if needed to reach a good spreading consistency.

6. Once the brownie base is completely cool, use a palette knife to spread the buttercream icing evenly over the top of the brownie.

7. To decorate, divide the white chocolate into two small, heatproof bowls. Add a few drops of green food coloring to one bowl and a few drops of orange to the other. Melt each colored chocolate separately in the microwave: cover the bowls and melt in short 10-second blasts on high power, stirring each time until the chocolate is smooth and melted (do not let it overheat).

8. Use a teaspoon to drizzle stripes of green and orange melted chocolate over the top of the iced brownies. Let the chocolate set before serving to ensure clean cuts. Slice into 9 equal pieces, then cut each piece into 4 small bites, and serve.

Fruit and Nut Granola Bar Brownie

The hearty goodness of a granola bar meets the indulgent, gooey texture of a chocolate brownie. The whole thing is studded with raisins and hazelnuts for extra flavor and crunch.

MAKES 9

¾ cup (175g) unsalted
  butter, diced

3½oz (100g) dark (70%)
  chocolate, broken into
  small pieces

1½ cups (300g) sugar

½ tsp vanilla extract or paste

¾ cup plus 1 tbsp (100g)
  all-purpose flour

½ tsp baking powder

3 eggs

**For the fruit and nut
granola bar base**

6 tbsp (100g) unsalted butter

½ cup (100g) light brown sugar

⅓ cup (85g) light corn syrup

2½ cups (245g) old-fashioned
  rolled oats

⅓ cup (45g) chopped hazelnuts

⅓ cup (50g) raisins

1. Begin with the fruit and nut granola bar base. In a saucepan, gently melt the butter over low heat. Once the butter is melted, remove the pan from the heat and stir in the sugar and corn syrup until fully combined. Add the oats, hazelnuts, and raisins to the mixture, then mix thoroughly until all ingredients are well coated.

2. Press this mixture evenly into the prepared baking pan to make a firm, compact layer. Set aside.

3. Preheat the oven to 350°F (180°C).

4. For the brownie, make the batter, following steps 2–4 of the Original Chocolate Brownie recipe (see p12).

5. To assemble, pour the brownie batter over the fruit and nut granola bar base, using a spatula to spread it out in an even layer.

6. Bake for 35–40 minutes. The brownie is done when the edges are set, and the center has risen and started to crack but may still look a bit soft and jiggly. Test with a toothpick (see step 6, p12).

7. Let cool completely in the pan on a wire rack for 1–2 hours. If you're in a hurry, pop the pan in the fridge for 30–45 minutes. Slice into 9 equal pieces and serve.

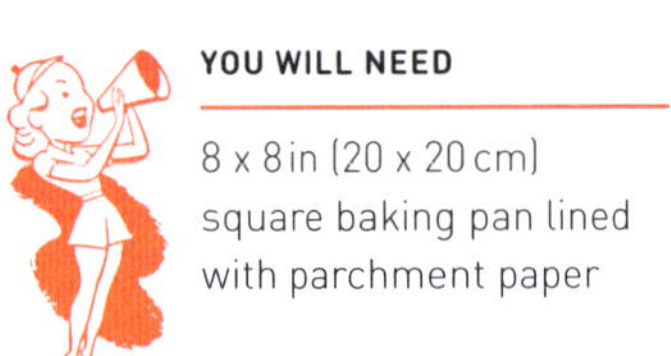

YOU WILL NEED

8 x 8 in (20 x 20 cm)
square baking pan lined
with parchment paper

"

Brownie Mince Pies

Mincemeat may not be on your holiday radar, but this premade mixture of candied fruit and spices blends perfectly with the rich filling of a chocolate brownie—all encased in ready-rolled shortcrust pastry—for a festive twist on the classic mince pie. Find mincemeat in the specialty section of the grocery store or the baking aisle. There will be some brownie base mixture left over—for a treat, pour it into a prepared baking pan and bake for 30 minutes.

MAKES 12

two 11¼oz (320g) premade
   pie crusts

¾ cup (175g) unsalted
   butter, diced

3½oz (100g) dark (70%)
   chocolate, broken into
   small pieces

1½ cups (300g) sugar

½ tsp vanilla extract or paste

¾ cup plus 1 tbsp (100g)
   all-purpose flour

½ tsp baking powder

3 eggs

10oz (300g) jar mincemeat

To finish

1 egg, beaten

demerara sugar, for sprinkling

powdered sugar, for dusting
   (optional)

1. Preheat the oven to 350°F (180°C).

2. Unroll the pastry onto a work surface. Using a 5in (12cm) round cutter, cut out 12 pastry bases. Press the bases firmly into each hole in the muffin pan. Set aside.

3. Make the brownie batter, following steps 2–4 of the Original Chocolate Brownie recipe (see p12).

4. Gently fold the mincemeat into the batter until it is evenly distributed. Spoon the brownie-mincemeat filling into the pie crusts, filling them almost to the top.

5. For a traditional mince pie look, use a 4in (10cm) pastry cutter to cut circles from the leftover pastry for lids, or to make decorative shapes (such as stars), sticking them on with some of the beaten egg. If making lids, place the lids on top of the filling, crimping the edges with the tines of a fork to seal, if you like. Brush with a little beaten egg for a golden finish, then sprinkle over demerara sugar for crunch.

6. Bake the pies for 20–25 minutes until the pastry has turned golden brown. Let cool completely in the muffin pan before carefully removing them. If you'd like, dust with powdered sugar before serving.

YOU WILL NEED

5in (12cm) and 4in (10cm)
round pastry cutters
12-hole muffin pan,
greased
Star-shaped pastry cutter
(optional)

Halloween Spiced Latte Brownie

The chocolate brownie takes on a spooky new dimension—infused with warming spices and topped with pumpkin-flavored icing and a marshmallow spiderweb.

MAKES 9

¾ cup (175g) unsalted
  butter, diced

¼ tsp ground cinnamon

¼ tsp ground ginger

1 tbsp instant espresso powder

3½oz (100g) dark (70%)
  chocolate, broken into
  small pieces

1½ cups (300g) sugar

½ tsp vanilla extract or paste

¾ cup plus 1 tbsp (100g)
  all-purpose flour

½ tsp baking powder

3 eggs

**For the pumpkin
buttercream icing**

5 tbsp (70g) unsalted butter,
  softened

2½ tbsp canned pumpkin

½ tsp ground cinnamon

½ tsp ground ginger

½ tsp ground cloves

2¼ cups (270g) powdered sugar

To decorate

6–8 large marshmallows

Halloween sprinkles

YOU WILL NEED

8 x 8in (20 x 20cm)
square baking pan lined
with parchment paper

1. Preheat the oven to 350°F (180°C).

2. Make the brownie batter, following steps 2–4 of the Original Chocolate Brownie recipe (see p12). Add the ¼ teaspoon cinnamon, ¼ teaspoon ginger, and espresso powder as the butter melts; these flavors will infuse into the brownies.

3. Pour the batter into the prepared baking pan. Bake for 35–40 minutes. It is done when the edges are set, and the center has risen and started to crack but may still look a bit soft and jiggly. Test with a toothpick (see step 6, p15). Let cool completely in the pan on a wire rack for 1–2 hours.

4. Meanwhile, make the pumpkin buttercream icing. In a bowl, combine the butter, canned pumpkin, cinnamon, ginger, and cloves and mix to combine. Sift in the powdered sugar gradually, one tablespoon at a time, and mix until the powdered sugar is fully incorporated and the icing is smooth. It may separate slightly to start but will come together as it thickens.

5. Chill the icing in the refrigerator for 30 minutes to let it firm up before decorating. Once the brownie is completely cool, remove it from the pan. Use a palette knife to spread the chilled icing evenly over the top.

6. For the marshmallow decoration, put the marshmallows in a large microwave-safe bowl. Cover and microwave the marshmallows in short, 10-second bursts, stirring in between until the mixture is melted, smooth, and sticky. Be careful, as the melted mixture will be very hot.

7. Set aside until cool enough to handle. To make the spiderweb decoration, scoop a blob of the cooled marshmallow, mash it between your fingers, then quickly pull your hands apart. This will stretch the marshmallow into thin, spiderweb-like strands. Drag this web across the surface of the brownie. Repeat this process until the web covers the area you'd like—usually 2 or 3 times is enough. Scatter over the Halloween sprinkles, slice into 9 equal pieces, and serve.

Welsh Cake Brownie

Fruity, spiced Welsh cakes—a traditional scone cooked on a flat griddle—are beloved by anyone who's visited Wales. Here, they combine beautifully with the signature gooey texture of the chocolate brownie base. Tradition with a unique twist.

MAKES 9

For the Welsh cake layer

⅔ cup (80g) all-purpose flour

1 tsp baking powder

¼ tsp salt

2½ tbsp sugar

3 tbsp unsalted butter, diced

¼ cup (40g) golden raisins

1 tsp pumpkin pie spice

For the brownie batter

¾ cup (175g) unsalted
 butter, diced

3½oz (100g) dark (70%)
 chocolate, broken into
 small pieces

1½ cups (300g) sugar,
 plus 2 tsp to serve

½ tsp vanilla extract or paste

¾ cup plus 1 tbsp (100g)
 all-purpose flour

½ tsp baking powder

3 eggs

1. Preheat the oven to 350°F (180°C).

2. Begin with the Welsh cake layer. In a medium bowl, combine the flour, baking powder, salt, and sugar. Add the butter. Using your fingertips, rub the butter into the flour and sugar until the mixture resembles fine breadcrumbs. Stir in the golden raisins and pumpkin pie spice. Press the Welsh cake mixture firmly and evenly into the base of the prepared baking pan to form a compacted base layer. Set aside.

3. Make the brownie batter, following steps 2–4 of the Original Chocolate Brownie recipe (see p12).

4. Pour the batter evenly over the Welsh cake layer.

5. Bake for 40 minutes. It is done when the edges are set, and the center has risen and started to crack but may still look a bit soft and jiggly. Test with a toothpick (see step 6, p12).

6. Let cool completely in the pan on a wire rack for 1–2 hours. To remove the brownie from the pan, turn the pan upside down and turn the brownie out so that the Welsh cake layer is at the top. Decorate by sprinkling over 2 teaspoons of sugar, then slice into 9 equal serving pieces.

YOU WILL NEED

8 x 8 in (20 x 20 cm) square baking pan lined with parchment paper

TIP

If you'd like, you can change or add different spices and flavorings to the Welsh cake layer. The ones I've tried and tested include ground cardamom, chopped candied ginger, and dried cranberries.

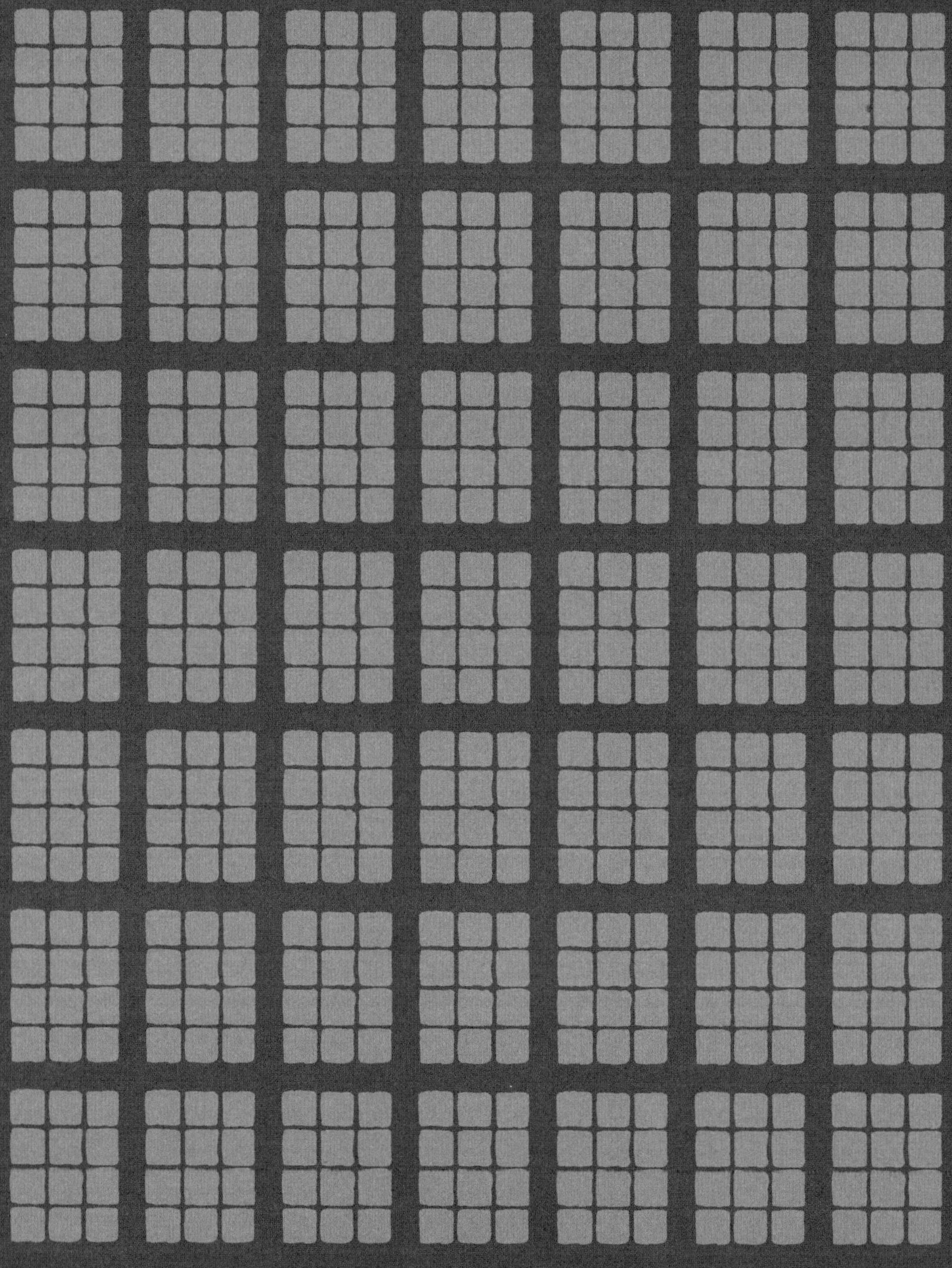

Blondies

The White Chocolate Blondie

My personal favorite, blondies. These taste sweeter and more buttery than the conventional brownies—they're the yin to the original brownie's yang. Once you've mastered this recipe, try the Hot Skillet Blondies (see right), add your favorite sauces (see right and p13), and explore the other fabulous blondie recipes in this chapter and beyond.

MAKES 9 BLONDIES

¾ cup (175g) unsalted
butter, diced

5½oz (150g) white chocolate,
broken into small pieces

1½ cups (300g) sugar

½ tsp vanilla extract or paste

1¼ cups (150g) all-purpose flour

½ tsp baking powder

3 eggs

YOU WILL NEED

8 x 8in (20 x 20 cm) square baking pan lined with parchment paper

TIPS

For the best fudgy texture, let the cooked blondies rest at room temperature overnight before portioning up.

If you're in a hurry, pop the cooked blondies in the fridge for 30–45 minutes to cool quickly.

1. Preheat the oven to 350°F (180°C).

2. Put a medium, heavy-based saucepan over medium heat. Add the butter and melt slowly, stirring continuously (be careful not to let it burn). Turn the heat to low, add the chocolate and, using a spatula, keep stirring until the chocolate has melted completely into the butter. It will look a little oily and almost split at this stage but keep stirring until you have a smooth, glossy mixture.

3. Take the pan off the heat. Add the sugar and vanilla to the pan and use a spatula to mix thoroughly. Add the flour and baking powder and mix into the wet ingredients until you have a yellow chocolatey mixture that resembles wet sand, with no lumps of flour or sugar visible.

4. In a medium bowl, whisk the eggs for 20–30 seconds until they're light and frothy. Using a large metal spoon, carefully fold the whisked eggs through the chocolate mixture, keeping as much air in the mixture as possible, to form a thick, smooth batter.

5. Pour the batter into the prepared pan, spreading it evenly over the base. Bake for 35 minutes. The blondie is done when the edges are set and the center has risen and started to crack but may still look a bit soft and jiggly.

6. Test with a toothpick. If it comes out completely covered in smooth batter, bake for a few minutes more. When it's perfectly cooked, the toothpick should come out with a few small clumps of batter sticking to it. If it comes out clean, the blondie will be more cake-like.

7. Let cool in the pan on a wire rack for 1–2 hours to reach the best texture (the blondies will continue to cook as they cool). Slice into 9 equal pieces and serve. The blondies can be stored in an airtight container for 10 days. They also freeze fabulously.

1. Follow steps 1–4, opposite. Pour the blondie batter into an 8 in (20 cm) skillet or oven-safe dish, lined with parchment paper, and bake for 25 minutes. The texture will still be soft.

2. Let cool in the skillet for about 20 minutes (it will be very hot straight from the oven).

3. Serve from the skillet and let everyone dig in, or spoon into separate bowls. If you like, top with a few scoops of good-quality vanilla ice cream, a few crumbled brownie pieces (from a previous batch), and drizzle over your favorite sauce (see below and p13).

YOU WILL NEED

8 in (20 cm) skillet or oven-safe dish lined with parchment paper

Boozy Dark Cherries in Syrup

1 x 14.5oz (410g) can pitted dark sweet cherries
3 tbsp plus 1 tsp (40g) sugar
3 tbsp plus 1 tsp (50ml) vodka

1. Drain the cherries, reserving the juice.

2. Put the juice and sugar in a small saucepan and boil to reduce the liquid to a thick, sticky, almost jam-like consistency.

3. Let cool for 20–30 minutes, then stir in the cherries and vodka.

Salted Caramel Sauce

½ cup (100g) light brown sugar
¾ cup (175ml) heavy cream
3 tbsp (50g) butter
1 tsp sea salt

1. Combine the sugar, cream, butter, and salt in a saucepan set over low heat, stirring until the sugar has dissolved.

2. Turn up the heat and bubble for 2–3 minutes until golden and syrupy.

3. Let cool slightly before serving.

Gluten-Free Blondie

A gluten-free recipe that has all the deliciousness of the classic white chocolate blondie. It's a wonderfully moist and rich treat.

MAKES 9

¾ cup (175g) unsalted
  butter, diced

5½oz (150g) white chocolate,
  broken into small pieces

1½ cups (300g) sugar

½ tsp vanilla extract or paste

1½ cups (180g) gluten-free
  bread flour

½ tsp baking powder

3 eggs

1. Preheat the oven to 350ºF (180ºC).

2. To make the blondie batter, follow steps 2–4 of the White Chocolate Blondie recipe (see p78).

3. Pour the batter into the prepared pan, spreading it evenly over the base. Bake for 40–45 minutes. It is done when the edges are set, and the center has risen and started to crack but may still look a bit soft and jiggly. Test with a toothpick (see step 6, p78).

4. Let cool completely in the pan on a wire rack for 1–2 hours. If you're in a hurry, pop the pan in the fridge for 30–45 minutes. Slice into 9 equal pieces and serve.

TIPS

Don't overmix the ingredients. Just simply combine, rather than beating them together.

We swear by using good-quality gluten-free flour, available at most supermarkets and grocery stores.

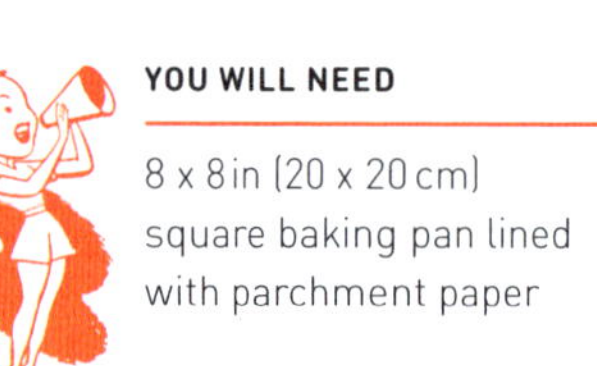

YOU WILL NEED

8 x 8 in (20 x 20 cm)
square baking pan lined
with parchment paper

Matcha Blondie

Matcha and white chocolate are a perfect match, and this blondie combo infuses the blondie with earthy matcha powder to create a visually striking and quite delicious treat, with an unusual flavor profile.

MAKES 12

¾ cup (175g) unsalted
  butter, diced

5½oz (150g) white chocolate,
  broken into small pieces

1½ cups (300g) sugar

½ tsp vanilla extract or paste

1¼ cups (150g) all-purpose flour

½ tsp baking powder

3 eggs

2 tbsp matcha powder

1. Preheat the oven to 350°F (180°C).

2. To make the blondie batter, follow steps 2–4 of the White Chocolate Blondie recipe (see p78).

3. Divide the prepared blondie batter evenly between two bowls. Add the matcha powder to one bowl and mix thoroughly until the batter is uniformly green and well combined. You now have an original blondie batter and a matcha blondie batter.

4. Let the batter rest for 10–15 minutes, then dollop alternating spoonfuls of the plain blondie batter and the green matcha blondie batter into the prepared baking pan. Continue until all the batter is used, creating an alternating green and white color effect.

5. Bake for 35–40 minutes. It is done when the edges are set and the center has risen and started to crack but may still look a bit soft and jiggly. Test with a toothpick (see step 6, p78).

6. Let cool completely in the pan on a wire rack for 1–2 hours. If you're in a hurry, pop the pan in the fridge for 30–45 minutes. Slice into 12 equal pieces and serve.

pictured overleaf >>

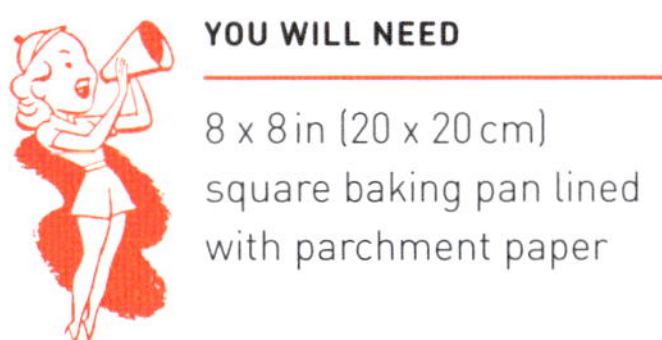

YOU WILL NEED

8 x 8 in (20 x 20 cm)
square baking pan lined
with parchment paper

Apple Crumble and Custard Blondie

Surely the ultimate comforting dessert for fall, made with a sweet and tangy apple puree. These make the perfect ending to a Sunday roast.

MAKES 9

For the apple compote

1¾ cups (400g) apple sauce (ensure it is thick; if it's watery, reduce in a pan over low heat until thickened and sticky)

1 tsp ground cinnamon

For the custard swirl

4½oz (125g) white chocolate

scant ⅓ cup (75ml) sour cream

2 tbsp vanilla extract or paste

1 egg

For the blondie batter

¾ cup (175g) unsalted butter, diced

5½oz (150g) white chocolate, broken into small pieces

1½ cups (300g) sugar

½ tsp vanilla extract or paste

1¼ cups (150g) all-purpose flour

½ tsp baking powder

3 eggs

1. Start with the apple compote and the first custard layer. Spread the apple sauce evenly over the base of the prepared pan. Sprinkle with cinnamon.

2. Next, prepare the custard swirl mixture. Put the chocolate in a medium microwave-safe bowl, cover, and carefully melt in short 10-second blasts on high power, stirring each time until the chocolate is smooth and melted (be very careful not to let it overheat). Add the sour cream and vanilla and mix well. Finally, beat in the egg using a spatula until well combined.

3. Spread half of the custard swirl mixture evenly over the apple layer in the baking pan. Put the pan into the freezer and freeze for 1–2 hours until solid. This step is crucial for creating distinct layers.

4. Preheat the oven to 350ºF (180ºC).

5. To make the blondie batter, follow steps 2–4 of the White Chocolate Blondie recipe (see p78).

6. Pour half of the prepared blondie batter into the second prepared baking pan, smoothing it evenly over the base. Take the frozen apple and custard layer from the freezer and carefully place it on top of this first layer of blondie batter. Pour the remaining blondie batter over the frozen layer, smoothing it out and ensuring the apple and custard layer is completely covered.

YOU WILL NEED

Two 8 x 8 in (20 x 20 cm) square baking pans lined with parchment paper

For the crumble topping

3 all-butter shortbread cookies

7. Spoon the remaining custard swirl mixture onto the top of the blondie batter and use a toothpick to swirl it through decoratively. For the crumble topping, break up the shortbread cookies into a mix of bigger pieces and light crumbs. Sprinkle this evenly over the top of the blondie.

8. Bake for 45–50 minutes. The blondie is done when the edges are set, and the center may have a very slight jiggle but is firm to touch. Test with a toothpick (see step 6, p78).

9. Let cool completely in the pan on a wire rack for 1–2 hours before slicing into 9 equal pieces and serving. Cooling completely is crucial for clean slices and for the layers to set properly.

pictured overleaf >>

TIP

Blackberries would be a good choice as an alternative to apples in this recipe. Their tartness would pair particularly well with the sweetness of the blondie.

Jam and Coconut Blondie

This recipe delivers a delightful blend of soft coconut blondie, a sweet jam layer, and a sprinkle of toasted coconut. Perfect for a comforting treat.

MAKES 9

¾ cup (175g) unsalted butter, diced

5½oz (150g) white chocolate, broken into small pieces

1½ cups (300g) sugar

½ tsp vanilla extract or paste

1¼ cups (150g) all-purpose flour

½ tsp baking powder

3 eggs

1 cup (75g) shredded, unsweetened coconut

For the topping

1–1¼ cups (250–300g) raspberry jam (or your favorite jam)

¼ cup (20g) shredded, unsweetened coconut (optional)

1. Preheat the oven to 350°F (180C).

2. Make the blondie batter, following steps 2–4 of the White Chocolate Blondie recipe (see p78).

3. Pour the batter into the prepared baking pan, spreading it evenly over the base. Bake for 35–40 minutes. It is done when the edges are set and the center has risen and started to crack but may still look a bit soft and jiggly. Test with a toothpick (see step 6, p78).

4. Let cool in the pan on a wire rack for about 5 minutes.

5. For the topping, while the blondie is still warm, give the raspberry jam a good stir to loosen it, then use a palette knife to spread it evenly over the top of the blondie. If using, sprinkle the shredded coconut evenly over the jam layer.

6. Let cool completely in the pan for 1–2 hours before slicing into 9 equal serving pieces. Cooling completely is crucial for clean slices and to allow the layers to set.

YOU WILL NEED

8 x 8 in (20 x 20 cm) square baking pan lined with parchment paper

Peanut Butter and Jelly Blondie

These take the luscious white chocolate blondie base and elevate it, with a delightful layer of peanut butter and strawberry jam.

MAKES 9

For the peanut butter and jelly layer

1 cup (250g) peanut butter (smooth or crunchy)

1 cup (250g) strawberry jam

For the blondie batter

¾ cup (175g) unsalted butter, diced

5½oz (150g) white chocolate, broken into small pieces

1½ cups (300g) sugar

½ tsp vanilla extract or paste

1¼ cups (150g) all-purpose flour

½ tsp baking powder

3 eggs

1. Start by making the peanut butter and jelly layer. Use a spatula to spread the peanut butter evenly into the base of a lined baking pan, creating a firm layer. Carefully spread the strawberry jam over the peanut butter layer. Put the pan with the peanut butter and jelly layers in the freezer for about 1 hour, until it is solid. This will make it easier to handle when layering in the blondie batter.

2. Preheat the oven to 350°F (180°C).

3. To make the blondie batter, follow steps 2–4 of the White Chocolate Blondie recipe (see p78).

4. To assemble, pour half of the prepared blondie batter into a second prepared baking pan. Take the frozen peanut butter and jelly layer from the freezer and carefully place it on top of this first layer of blondie batter.

5. Pour the remaining blondie batter over the frozen layer, ensuring the middle layer is completely covered. Bake for 40–45 minutes.

6. It is done when the edges are set, and the center has risen and started to crack but may still look a bit soft and jiggly. Test with a toothpick (see step 6, p78).

7. Let cool completely in the pan on a wire rack for 1–2 hours. If you're in a hurry, pop the pan in the fridge for 30–45 minutes. Slice into 9 equal pieces and serve.

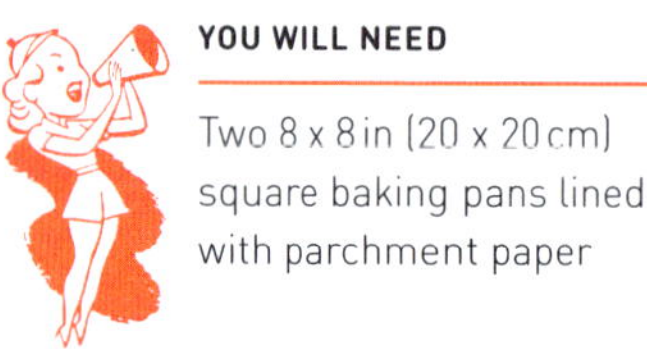

YOU WILL NEED

Two 8 x 8 in (20 x 20 cm) square baking pans lined with parchment paper

White Chocolate Bakewell Blondie

Bakewell tarts are a British classic layered with jam and almonds—here in blondie form—featuring the sweetness of the jam and a crunchy nutty topping to give a little more texture.

MAKES 9

¾ cup (175g) unsalted
  butter, diced

5½oz (150g) white chocolate,
  broken into small pieces

1½ cups (300g) sugar

½ tsp vanilla extract or paste

1¼ cups (150g) all-purpose flour

1¾oz (50g) ground almonds

½ tsp baking powder

3 eggs

1 x 11¼oz (320g) premade
  pie crust

3 tbsp raspberry jam

3 tbsp sliced almonds

1. Preheat the oven to 350°F (180°C).

2. To make the blondie batter, follow steps 2–4 of the White Chocolate Blondie recipe (see p78).

3. Roll out the pie crust so that it is large enough to fit into the base of the baking pan. Prick the base of the pastry all over with a fork.

4. Loosely fit another sheet of parchment paper inside the pan, over the crust, and pour in the ceramic pie weights to cover the base. Blind bake the pastry for 15 minutes, then set aside to cool. Keep the oven on.

5. Once cooled, remove the ceramic pie weights and parchment paper, and evenly spread the raspberry jam over the pastry to give a nice, thick layer. Carefully pour the blondie batter over the pastry and jam layers, spreading it out evenly. Sprinkle the sliced almonds evenly over the top of the blondie batter.

6. Bake for 30 minutes. It is done when the edges of the blondie are set, and the center has risen and started to crack but may still look a bit soft and jiggly. Test with a toothpick (see step 6, p78).

7. Let cool completely in the pan on a wire rack for 1–2 hours. If you're in a hurry, pop the pan in the fridge for 30–45 minutes. Slice into 9 equal pieces and serve.

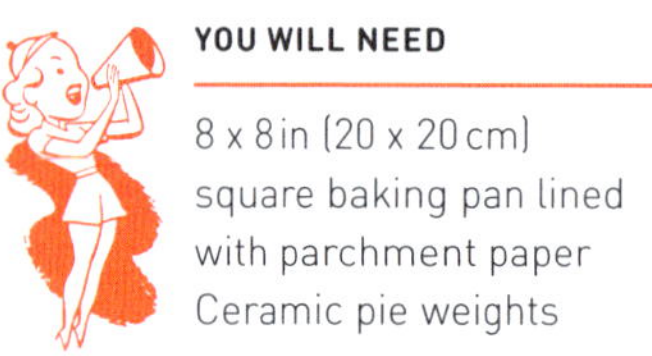

YOU WILL NEED

8 x 8 in (20 x 20 cm)
square baking pan lined
with parchment paper
Ceramic pie weights

Caramel Apple Upside-Down Blondie

The gorgeously gooey combination of buttery caramel and baked apples is unbeatable. I've turned that idea into an upside-down topping for a blondie base.

MAKES 9

For the apple caramel topping

6 tbsp (90g) unsalted butter

scant 1 cup (100g) light or dark brown sugar

¼ tsp ground cinnamon

¼ tsp vanilla extract or paste

2 medium apples (6¾–9oz/190–250g), peeled, cored, and cut into ¼in (5mm) slices

For the blondie batter

¾ cup (175g) unsalted butter, diced

5½oz (150g) white chocolate, broken into small pieces

1½ cups (300g) sugar

½ tsp vanilla extract or paste

1¼ cups (150g) all-purpose flour

½ tsp baking powder

3 eggs

1. Start with the apple caramel topping. Combine the butter and sugar in a small saucepan over medium heat, whisking occasionally until the butter has melted. When the mixture begins to thicken, whisk constantly for 1 minute, until you have a light brown, sticky caramel.

2. Remove the caramel from the heat and whisk in the ground cinnamon and vanilla. Arrange the apple slices neatly in the bottom of the lined pan, overlapping where necessary. Carefully pour the caramel over the apples. Put the pan in the refrigerator for a few minutes while you prepare the blondie batter; chilling will help solidify and set the topping.

3. Preheat the oven to 350°F (180°C).

4. To make the blondie batter, follow steps 2–4 of the White Chocolate Blondie recipe (see p78).

5. Remove the pan with the prepared topping from the refrigerator. Pour the blondie batter evenly over the apple and caramel topping in the pan, smoothing it out to the edges, being careful not to disturb the apples.

6. Bake for 45–50 minutes. The blondie is done when the edges are set, and the center has risen and started to crack but may still look a bit soft and jiggly. Test with a toothpick (see step 6, p78).

7. Remove the blondie from the oven and cool in the pan on a wire rack for just 15 minutes.

8. Carefully invert the slightly cooled blondie onto a cake stand or serving plate. Some of the juices from the topping may seep over the sides, which is normal.

9. For the cleanest slices, it is best to cool the blondie completely at room temperature before slicing into 9 equal serving pieces. Do not refrigerate to speed up the cooling process, as this could make the blondie overly dense.

YOU WILL NEED

8 x 8in (20 x 20cm) square baking pan lined with parchment paper

Jaffa Cake Blondie

Jaffa cakes are classic cookies with orange and chocolate layers. I've layered the white chocolate blondie base with the signature orange gelatin, topped with dark chocolate.

MAKES 9

¾ cup (175g) unsalted
  butter, diced

finely grated zest of
  1 unwaxed orange

5½oz (150g) white chocolate,
  broken into small pieces

1½ cups (300g) sugar

½ tsp vanilla extract or paste

1¼ cups (150g)
  all-purpose flour

½ tsp baking powder

3 eggs

For the orange layer

4¾oz (135g) gelatin mix from
  6oz (170g) package orange-
  flavored gelatin dessert mix

juice of 2 unwaxed oranges,
  finely grated zest of 1

2 tbsp apricot jam

For the chocolate topping

8oz (230g) dark (50%) chocolate,
  broken into small pieces

1 tbsp neutral vegetable oil

YOU WILL NEED

Two 8 x 8 in (20 x 20 cm)
square baking pans lined
with parchment paper

1. Preheat the oven to 350°F (180°C). To make the blondie batter, follow steps 2–4 of the White Chocolate Blondie recipe (see p78). Add the orange zest to the butter as it melts to help infuse the orange flavor throughout the blondies.

2. Pour the batter into a prepared baking pan, spreading it evenly over the base. Bake for 35–40 minutes. It is done when the edges are set and the center has risen and started to crack but may still look a bit soft and jiggly. Test with a toothpick (see step 6, p78). Let cool completely in the pan on a wire rack for 1–2 hours.

3. Meanwhile, prepare the orange gelatin layer. Put the orange gelatin mix into a small heatproof bowl. Pour the orange juice into a heatproof measuring jug. Add boiling water to make up ⅔ cup (150ml) of liquid and pour the hot liquid over the orange gelatin mix, stirring until it is completely dissolved. Stir in the orange zest. Pour enough of the orange gelatin mixture into the second prepared baking pan to cover the base to a depth of ¼in (5mm). Chill in the fridge for 1 hour, or until firmly set.

4. Meanwhile, for the chocolate topping, put the dark chocolate in a heatproof, microwave-safe bowl, cover, and carefully melt in short 10-second blasts on high power, stirring each time until the chocolate is smooth and melted (be very careful not to overheat). Stir in the oil and let the chocolate cool and thicken slightly.

5. To assemble, once the blondie base is completely cool, spread the apricot jam thinly over the top. Remove the set gelatin layer from its pan, using the parchment paper to help you. Place the gelatin layer on top of the apricot jam layer. Gently spoon the melted chocolate over the gelatin layer and use a palette knife to smooth it out, being careful not to rip the gelatin.

6. Let set completely until the chocolate has hardened, about 1 hour, before removing from the pan. Using a sharp knife to help prevent the chocolate from cracking, cut into 9 equal serving pieces.

pictured overleaf >>

Carrot Cake Blondie

Moist, dense, and nutty, this sweet treat builds on the blondie base, adding warming spices and the earthy sweetness of carrots—and it's all topped off with a smooth, tangy cream cheese frosting. Irresistible.

MAKES 9

2–3 medium (150g) carrots

¾ cup (175g) unsalted
  butter, diced

1½ tsp ground cinnamon
  (see tip, p102)

5½oz (150g) white chocolate,
  broken into small pieces

1½ cups (300g) sugar

½ tsp vanilla extract or paste

1¼ cups (150g) all-purpose flour

½ tsp baking powder

3 eggs

½ cup (50g) chopped walnuts,
  lightly toasted, plus extra to
  serve (optional)

1. Preheat the oven to 350°F (180°C).

2. Peel and finely grate the carrots then squeeze out as much juice as possible using a clean dish towel.

3. To make the blondie batter, follow steps 2–4 of the White Chocolate Blondie recipe (see p78). Add the ground cinnamon (and any other optional warming spices; see tip, p102) to the melting butter to help infuse the flavor throughout the blondies.

4. In a medium bowl, whisk the eggs for 20–30 seconds until they're light and frothy. Using a large metal spoon, carefully fold the whisked eggs through the chocolate mixture, keeping as much air in the mixture as possible, to form a smooth, thick batter.

5. Gently fold the grated carrots and the chopped walnuts (if using) into the batter until just combined. Be careful not to overmix, as this can deflate the batter.

6. Pour the batter into the prepared baking pan, spreading it evenly over the base. Bake for 40–45 minutes. It is done when the edges are set, and the center has risen and started to crack but may still look a bit soft and jiggly. Test with a toothpick (see step 6, p78).

recipe continues >>

YOU WILL NEED

8 x 8 in (20 x 20 cm)
square baking pan lined
with parchment paper
Electric hand whisk,
or mixer fitted with
a paddle attachment

For the cream cheese frosting

5 tbsp (75g) unsalted butter, softened

5½oz (150g) full-fat cream cheese, softened (ensure it is brick-style, not spreadable, and at room temperature)

1⅔ cups (200g) powdered sugar, sifted

1 tsp vanilla extract or paste

1 tbsp lemon juice (optional)

7. Let cool completely in the pan on a wire rack for at least 1–2 hours, or until the base of the pan feels cool to the touch. This is important before adding the frosting.

8. Meanwhile, make the cream cheese frosting. In a mixer fitted with the paddle attachment (or in a large mixing bowl using an electric hand whisk), beat together the butter and cream cheese until smooth, creamy, and lump-free. Gradually add the powdered sugar 1 large spoonful at a time, beating until completely incorporated and smooth.

9. Add the vanilla and lemon juice, if using (the lemon will cut the sweetness and add a tangy complement). Beat until the frosting is smooth and well-combined. If it gets too warm and seems loose, put the bowl in the refrigerator to chill, then beat again.

10. Once the blondie carrot cake is completely cool, use a palette knife to spread the cream cheese frosting evenly over the top. Scatter more chopped walnuts over the frosting for decoration, if desired. Slice into 9 equal pieces and serve.

TIP

For even warmer spicing, use 1 teaspoon ground cinnamon, ½ teaspoon ground ginger, and ¼ teaspoon ground nutmeg or clove in place of the 1½ teaspoons ground cinnamon.

Far Breton Blondie

Far Breton is a traditional baked custard and prune dessert from Brittany in France. For a similar flavor, I've added prunes to our white chocolate blondie base, and created something rich, moist, and tender. It's baked slowly for a delightful texture.

SERVES 9

For the prunes

4¼oz (120g) drained pitted prunes (from a can or dried prunes, soaked)

¼ cup (50ml) Armagnac (optional; see tip)

For the blondie batter

¾ cup (175g) unsalted butter, diced

5½oz (150g) white chocolate, broken into small pieces

1½ cups (300g) sugar

½ tsp vanilla extract or paste

1¼ cups (150g) all-purpose flour

½ tsp baking powder

3 eggs

1. If you are using Armagnac (see tip, below), begin with the prunes. Put the prunes in a bowl. Pour over the Armagnac and let soak overnight. The next day, drain, reserving 1½ tablespoons (25ml) for the blondie mixture. If you are not using Armagnac, just skip this step.

2. Preheat the oven to 240°F (120°C).

3. To make the blondie batter, follow steps 2–4 of the White Chocolate Blondie recipe (see p78). If you soaked the prunes in Armagnac, add the reserved liquid to the blondie batter and mix until just combined.

4. Arrange the prunes evenly in the base of the prepared pan. Pour the blondie batter over the prunes in the pan, smoothing it out evenly and ensuring the prunes are fully covered. Bake in the middle of the preheated oven for about 2 hours, or until the blondie has set.

5. Let cool completely in the pan, at least 2 hours, before removing from the pan. Cut into 9 equal slices and serve.

pictured overleaf >>

YOU WILL NEED

8 in (20 cm) round cake pan lined with parchment paper

TIP

If you are soaking the prunes in Armagnac, follow step 1 the night before you bake.

Dubai Chocolate Pistachio Blondie

We have recreated the famous Dubai chocolate here by combining the white chocolate blondie base with the vibrant flavors and textures of this popular treat.

MAKES 9

¾ cup (175g) unsalted butter, diced

5½oz (150g) white chocolate, broken into small pieces

1½ cups (300g) sugar

½ tsp vanilla extract or paste

1¼ cups (150g) all-purpose flour

½ tsp baking powder

3 eggs

2½oz (75g) roasted *kataifi* pastry (see tip)

2½oz (75g) unsalted pistachios, chopped, plus extra to decorate

3½oz (100g) milk chocolate, for the topping

1. Preheat the oven to 350°F (180°C). To make the blondie batter, follow steps 2–4 of the White Chocolate Blondie recipe (see p78). Gently fold the *kataifi* pastry and pistachios into the blondie batter until just combined. Pour the batter into the prepared baking pan, spreading it evenly over the base.

2. Bake for 40–45 minutes. It is done when the edges are set, and the center has risen and started to crack but may still look a bit soft and jiggly. Test with a toothpick (see step 6, p78). Let cool completely in the pan on a wire rack for 1–2 hours.

3. Once the blondie has cooled, melt the milk chocolate for the topping. Put the chocolate in a microwave-safe bowl, cover, and melt in short 10-second blasts on high power, stirring each time until the chocolate is smooth and melted (do not let it overheat).

4. Pour the melted chocolate evenly over the cooled blondie in the pan, using a palette knife to spread it over the top. Immediately sprinkle additional chopped pistachios over the melted chocolate topping before it sets.

5. Let the chocolate topping cool and set completely before slicing the blondie into 9 equal serving pieces.

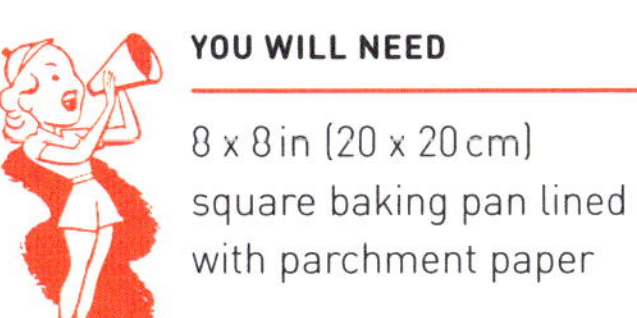

YOU WILL NEED

8 x 8 in (20 x 20 cm) square baking pan lined with parchment paper

TIP

Kataifi *pastry is a type of finely spun pastry strands, used in sweet and savory dishes in the Middle East. You can buy dried, roasted* kataifi *from Middle Eastern grocers or online.*

Valentine's Blondie

The addition of fresh raspberries and crunchy macadamia nuts transforms the white chocolate blondie base into a Valentine's Day treat. The whole thing is finished off with a delicate buttercream and romantic decorations.

MAKES 9

¾ cup (175g) unsalted
  butter, diced

5½oz (150g) white chocolate,
  broken into small pieces

1½ cups (300g) sugar

½ tsp vanilla extract or paste

1¼ cups (150g) all-purpose flour

½ tsp baking powder

3 eggs

½ cup (50g) macadamia
  nuts, chopped

3½oz (100g) white chocolate,
  broken into large chunks

3½oz (100g) raspberries, halved

For the buttercream

½ cup (125g) unsalted
  butter, softened

2½ cups (300g) powdered sugar

1 tbsp milk (more as needed)

2 tsp vanilla extract or paste

To decorate

your choice of whole fresh
  raspberries, heart-shaped
  candy sprinkles, dried edible
  flower petals, and/or white
  chocolate shavings

1. Preheat the oven to 350°F (180°C).

2. To make the blondie batter, follow steps 2–4 of the White Chocolate Blondie recipe (see p78).

3. Gently fold in the macadamia nuts, white chocolate chunks, and halved raspberries until just combined, being careful not to overmix. Pour the batter into the prepared baking pan, spreading it evenly over the base.

4. Bake for 40–45 minutes. It is done when the edges are set, and the center has risen and started to crack but may still look a bit soft and jiggly. Test with a toothpick (see step, 6, p78).

5. Let cool completely in the pan on a wire rack for 1–2 hours. The blondies will carry on cooking as they cool.

6. Meanwhile, make the buttercream. In a bowl, cream the butter until light and fluffy. Sift in the powdered sugar and carefully mix until fully incorporated and smooth. Add the milk and vanilla and mix until smooth, adding a bit more milk if necessary to reach a suitable spreading consistency.

7. Once the blondie is cool, spread the buttercream evenly over the top using a palette knife. Decorate with your choice of toppings. Slice into 9 equal pieces and serve.

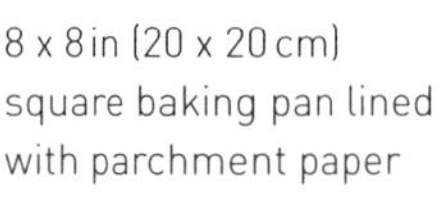

YOU WILL NEED

8 x 8 in (20 x 20 cm)
square baking pan lined
with parchment paper

Lemon Meringue Pie Blondie

The concept of combining lemon meringue pie with a blondie may seem novel (and it is) but the flavors work beautifully together, with a bright lemon blondie base, a tart lemon curd filling, and a fluffy meringue topping. An extraordinary, visually stunning dessert.

MAKES 9

¾ cup (175g) unsalted
  butter, diced

finely grated zest of
  1 unwaxed lemon

5½oz (150g) white chocolate,
  broken into small pieces

1½ cups (300g) sugar

½ tsp vanilla extract or paste

1¼ cups (150g) all-purpose flour

½ tsp baking powder

3 eggs

For the graham cracker base

7oz (200g) graham crackers

5 tbsp (75g) unsalted
  butter, melted

YOU WILL NEED

Food processor (optional)
8 x 8 in (20 x 20 cm)
square baking pan lined
with parchment paper
Mixer or electric
hand whisk
Kitchen blowtorch
(optional)

1. Preheat the oven to 350°F (180°C).

2. Start with the graham cracker base. Crush the graham crackers into fine crumbs using a food processor or by placing them in a sealed bag and crushing with a rolling pin.

3. Combine the graham cracker crumbs and melted butter in a bowl, mixing until the crumbs are evenly coated. Press this mixture firmly and evenly into the base of the prepared baking pan using the back of a spoon to compact it evenly. Let cool.

4. To make the blondie batter, follow steps 2–4 of the White Chocolate Blondie recipe (see p78). Add the lemon zest to the butter as it melts to help infuse the flavor throughout the blondies.

5. Pour the blondie batter over the cooled graham cracker crust in the baking pan, spreading it evenly over the graham cracker layer.

6. Bake for 35–40 minutes. It is done when the edges are set, and the center has risen and started to crack but may still look a bit soft and jiggly. Test with a toothpick (see step 6, p78).

7. Let the blondie cool completely in the pan on a wire rack for at least 2 hours, or until the bottom of the pan is cool to the touch. Once it has cooled completely, take it out of the pan.

8. Meanwhile, make the lemon curd layer. Gently warm the lemon curd in a small saucepan (or in a microwave) until it is slightly steamy or hot to the touch. This will help prevent the meringue from separating from the curd. Spread the warmed lemon curd evenly over the top of the cooled blondie layer.

For lemon curd layer and meringue topping

¾ cup (175g) lemon curd, from a jar

½ cup (100g) sugar

1 tbsp cornstarch

6 large egg whites (at room temperature for the best volume)

¼ tsp cream of tartar

½ tsp vanilla extract or paste

9. For the meringue topping, in a small bowl, whisk together the sugar and cornstarch.

10. In a clean bowl of a mixer (or in a large mixing bowl and using an electric hand whisk), put the egg whites, cream of tartar, and ½ teaspoon of vanilla. Ensure the bowl is spotlessly clean, as any grease can prevent egg whites from whisking properly.

11. Turn the mixer to medium speed and mix until the whites are frothy, then turn to high speed. Once the egg whites start to thicken and turn paler, begin adding the sugar/cornstarch mixture 1 tablespoon at a time, with the mixer running. You only need to wait a few seconds between additions. Continue mixing until the meringue is shiny and just holds stiff peaks when the whisk is removed from the bowl. Be careful not to over-whip, as this can result in an overly airy meringue.

12. To assemble, carefully spoon the meringue over the lemon curd layer. Start by placing spoonfuls around the edge of the blondie, then fill in the middle, building a mound on top. Ensure the meringue is spread out to the edges to seal it and prevent it from shrinking and pulling away during baking and cooling. Use the back of a spoon to create decorative swirls or peaks on the meringue.

13. Brown the meringue topping using a kitchen blowtorch. Or, heat the broiler to medium, transfer the blondie to a baking pan, and broil the meringue for 45 seconds to 1 minute, until it is a light golden brown. Watch the whole time, as it can burn quickly.

14. To cut clean slices, dip a sharp knife into hot water before each cut, wiping the knife clean and dipping it into hot water again before cutting. This is best enjoyed the day it's made, but leftovers can be stored lightly covered in the refrigerator for a few days, although the meringue may soften.

pictured overleaf >>

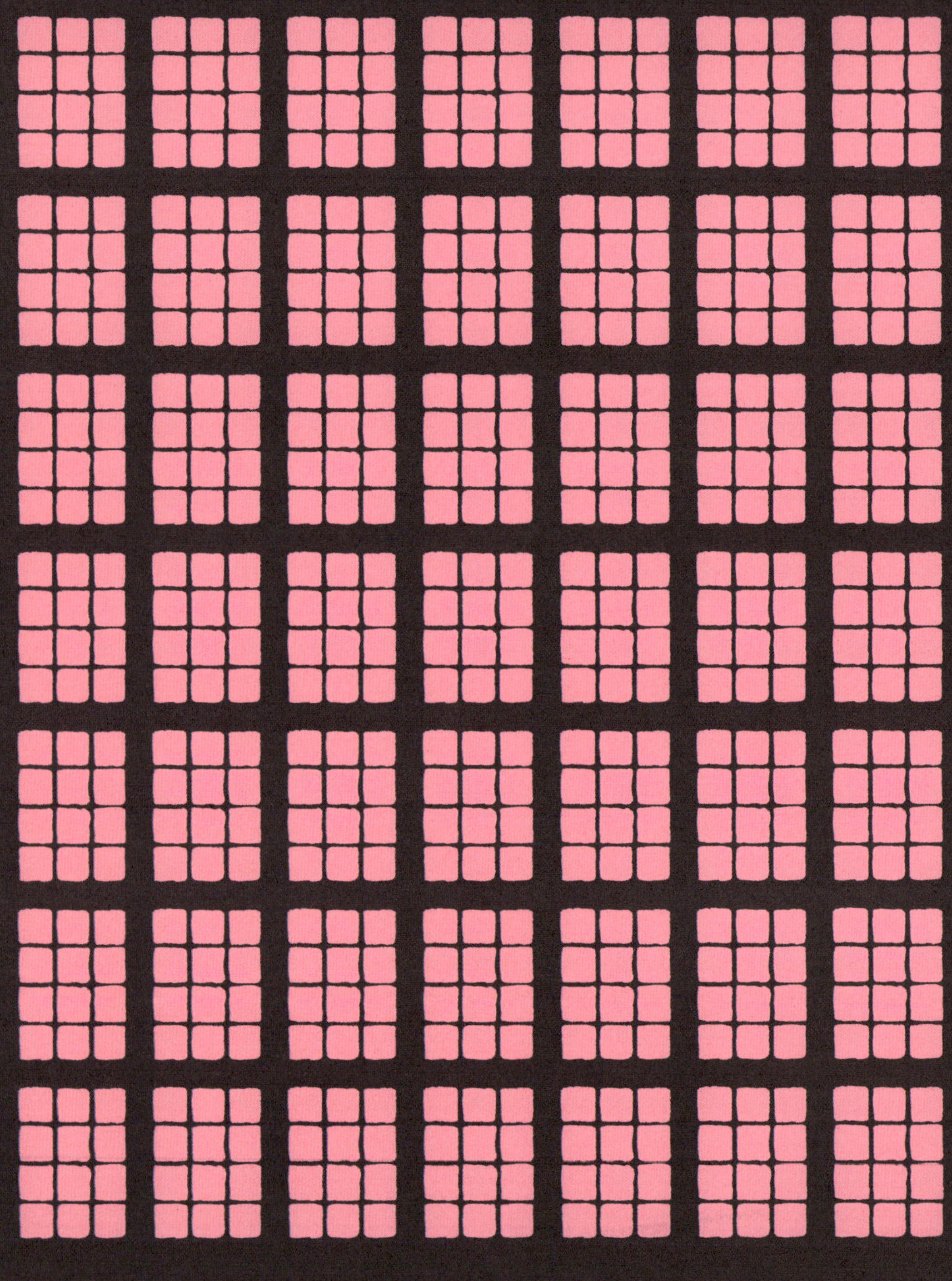

Beyond Brownies

Black Forest Brownie Tower

This is my re-imagination of that kitsch dessert that seemed to be everywhere in the 1980s. Using our classic brownie base, it's an easy one to put together and enjoy those memories.

SERVES 16

1 cup plus 7 tbsp (350g) unsalted butter, diced

7oz (200g) dark (70%) chocolate, broken into small pieces

3 cups (600g) sugar

1 tsp vanilla extract or paste

1⅔ cups (200g) all-purpose flour

1 tsp baking powder

6 eggs

To assemble, decorate, and serve

13oz (370g) jar whole black cherries in syrup

8 tbsp cherry jam

2½ cups (600ml) heavy cream

3½oz (100g) dark (70%) chocolate, for the chocolate curls

1. Preheat the oven to 350°F (180°C.

2. To make the two brownie rounds, follow steps 2–4 of the Original Chocolate Brownie recipe (see p12).

3. Divide the batter between the two prepared cake pans, spreading it evenly over the bases. Bake for 30–35 minutes. They are done when the edges are set, and the center has risen and started to crack but may still look a bit soft and jiggly. Test with a toothpick (see step 6, p12). Let both brownie rounds cool completely in their pans on a wire rack for 1–2 hours before removing them from the pans.

4. To assemble the brownie tower, put a brownie round on a serving plate. Spoon 4 tablespoons of the syrup from the jar (reserving the cherries) and drizzle over the top of the brownie. Using a spatula, spread the cherry jam over the brownie base.

5. In a medium bowl, use an electric hand whisk to whisk the cream until it just forms stiff peaks when the whisk is removed. Spread half the whipped cream over the cherry jam. Carefully place the second brownie round on top of the whipped cream. Spread the remaining whipped cream on top of the brownie tower.

6. To decorate, working directly over the tower, drag a vegetable peeler down the length of the edge of the chocolate bar to create small chocolate curls. Arrange the black cherries from the jar on top.

7. Using a sharp chef's knife, dip the blade into hot water and immediately wipe it completely dry. This is the secret to a clean cut, as the heat melts the chocolate, preventing it from sticking. Make a single, clean cut through the tower. Repeat the "heat and dry" step before each new slice.

YOU WILL NEED

Two 8in (20cm) round cake pans lined with parchment paper
Electric hand whisk

Jam and Cream Blondie Tower

Who doesn't love jam and cream together? Not sure you can beat delving into a decadent, buttery, white-chocolate blondie layered cake with a jam and cream filling. Perfect for afternoon tea, pull out your china teacups, and enjoy.

SERVES 18

1 cup plus 7 tbsp (350g) unsalted butter, diced

10oz (300g) white chocolate, broken into small pieces

3 cups (600g) sugar

1 tsp vanilla extract or paste

2¼ cups (300g) all-purpose flour

1 tsp baking powder

6 eggs

1 cup (200g) raspberry jam

For the buttercream

4 tbsp (50g) unsalted butter, softened

scant 1 cup (120g) powdered sugar, plus extra to decorate

1–2 tbsp milk

⅓ tsp vanilla extract or paste

1. Preheat the oven to 350°F (180°C).

2. For the blondie rounds, make the batter following steps 2–4 of the White Chocolate Blondie recipe (see p78).

3. Divide the batter equally between the prepared pans, spreading it evenly over the bases. Bake for 35–40 minutes. They are done when the edges are set, and the center has risen and started to crack, but may still look a bit soft and jiggly. Test with a toothpick (see step 6, p78). Let the blondie rounds cool in their pans on a wire rack for 1–2 hours before removing them from their pans.

4. Meanwhile, for the buttercream, in a medium bowl, use a spatula to beat the butter for 2–3 minutes until light and fluffy. Sift in the powdered sugar and carefully mix until fully incorporated and smooth. Add the milk and vanilla and mix again until smooth.

5. Once the blondie rounds have cooled, if they are uneven or dipped in the middle, you may wish to trim the tops with a serrated bread knife or cake leveler (if you have one) to give an even surface.

6. To assemble, place one blondie round on a serving plate. Use a palette knife to spread the buttercream evenly over the top of this first layer. Carefully spread the raspberry jam over the buttercream. Gently place the second blondie round on top of the jam layer. Decorate by sifting the powdered sugar over the top to give an even dusting.

7. Using a sharp chef's knife, dip the blade into hot water and immediately wipe it completely dry. This is the secret to a clean cut, as the heat prevents sticking. Make a single, clean cut through the tower. Repeat the "heat and dry" step before each new slice.

YOU WILL NEED

Two 8 in (20 cm) round baking pans lined with parchment paper
Cake leveler (optional)

Birthday Tower Blondie

Make a wish... I've re-imagined the white chocolate blondie recipe to create two festive, sprinkle-filled rounds, layered with raspberry jam and vanilla buttercream. Put it all together, decorate as you like, and you have a beautifully celebratory tower.

SERVES 18

1 cup plus 7 tbsp (350g)
  unsalted butter, diced

10oz (300g) white chocolate,
  broken into small pieces

3 cups (600g) sugar

1 tsp vanilla extract or paste

2¼ cups (300g) all-purpose flour

1 tsp baking powder

6 eggs

7oz (200g) sprinkles, plus
  extra to serve

4 tbsp raspberry jam

For the vanilla buttercream

1 stick plus 4 tbsp (160g)
  unsalted butter, softened

2⅓ cups (330g) powdered sugar

1 tsp vanilla extract or paste

2 tbsp milk

YOU WILL NEED

Two 8in (20cm) round
baking pans lined with
parchment paper
Cake leveler (optional)

1. Preheat the oven to 350°F (180°C).

2. For the blondie rounds, make the batter following steps 2–4 of the White Chocolate Blondie recipe (see p78). At the end of step 4, gently fold in the sprinkles until just combined.

3. Divide the batter equally between the prepared pans, spreading it evenly over the bases. Bake for 35–40 minutes. They are done when the edges are set, and the center has risen and started to crack, but may still look a bit soft and jiggly. Test with a toothpick (see step 6, p78). Let the blondie rounds cool in their pans on a wire rack for 1–2 hours before removing them from the pans.

4. Meanwhile, for the vanilla buttercream, in a bowl, use a spatula to beat the butter until light and fluffy. Sift in the powdered sugar and carefully mix until fully incorporated and smooth. Add the vanilla and milk, then mix again until smooth.

5. Once the blondie rounds have cooled, if they are uneven or dipped in the middle, you may wish to trim the tops with a serrated bread knife or cake leveler (if you have one) to give an even surface.

6. To assemble, place one blondie round on a serving plate or cake stand. Spread the raspberry jam evenly over the top of this first layer. Use a palette knife to carefully spread one-third of the prepared buttercream evenly over the jam layer.

7. Gently place the second blondie round on top of the buttercream layer. Spread another third of the buttercream evenly over the top of the blondie tower, then spread the rest of the buttercream (the final third) around the sides of the assembled tower, covering it completely. Finish the top of the tower with a final sprinkling of cake sprinkles, then add candles and any other decorations.

8. To serve, using a sharp chef's knife, dip the blade into hot water and immediately wipe it completely dry. This is the secret to a clean cut, as the heat prevents sticking. Make a single, clean cut through the tower. Repeat the "heat and dry" step before each new slice.

Death by Chocolate Brownie Tower

This is one of my absolute favorites: a classic chocolate brownie base built up into a luxurious, multilayered tower that truly lives up to its name. My philosophy is all about taking a great base and elevating it with simple yet transformative additions to create something spectacular.

SERVES 16

2 cups plus 2 tbsp (525g)
   unsalted butter, diced

10oz (300g) dark (70%)
   chocolate, broken into
   small pieces

4½ cups (900g) sugar

1½ tsp vanilla extract or paste

2¼ cups (300g) all-purpose flour

1½ tsp baking powder

9 eggs

dark (70%) chocolate shavings,
   to decorate (optional)

For the chocolate ganache

scant 1 cup (200ml)
   heavy cream

14oz (400g) dark (70%)
   chocolate, broken into
   small pieces

For the buttercream filling

½ cup plus 5 tbsp (200g)
   butter, softened

3½ cups (400g) powdered sugar

YOU WILL NEED

Three 8 in (20 cm)
round baking pans lined
with parchment paper
Instant-read thermometer
Cake leveler (optional)

1. Preheat the oven to 350°F (180°C).

2. For the brownie rounds, make the batter following steps 2–4 of the Original Chocolate Brownie recipe (see p12).

3. Pour one-third of the batter into each of the prepared baking pans, spreading it evenly over the bases. Bake for 30–35 minutes. They are done when the edges are set, and the center has risen and started to crack, but may still look a bit soft and jiggly. Test with a toothpick (see step 6, p12).

4. Let the brownie rounds cool in their pans on a wire rack for 1–2 hours before removing them from their pans. If your brownie rounds are uneven or dipped in the middle, you might want to trim the top using a serrated bread knife (or cake leveler if you have one) to make the assembly easier. Reserve the trimmings to make brownie crumbs for decorating, if you like.

5. To make the chocolate ganache, heat the cream in a pan over medium heat until it reaches 195°F (90°C) on an instant-read thermometer. The cream will begin to steam, but do not let it boil. Put the chocolate in a heatproof bowl, pour the hot cream over it, and let stand for 2 minutes. Using a spatula, mix the chocolate into the cream until well combined, smooth, and glossy. If the chocolate is not completely melted, cover the bowl and microwave for 5–10 seconds at full power, then mix again. Set aside.

6. To make the buttercream filling, put the butter in a medium bowl, then sift in the powdered sugar. Using a spatula, carefully mix the powdered sugar and butter until smooth. Add ⅓ cup (100g) of the chocolate ganache mixture (reserve the remainder for the topping) and mix again until you have a nice, smooth, light-brown buttercream thick enough to stand a spoon in.

recipe continues >>

7. To assemble the brownie tower, place the first brownie round on a serving plate or cake board. Using a spatula, spread one-third of the chocolate buttercream over the top. Place a second brownie round on top of this layer and evenly spread over another one-third of the chocolate buttercream. Place the third brownie round on top and evenly spread over the last of the chocolate buttercream.

8. Spread the reserved chocolate ganache in an even layer over the top and sides of the assembled tower. As the sides of the brownies are always a little rough and tumble, we'd suggest going a bit rustic and not too fussy with the decoration. Be as creative as you like. You can use dark chocolate shavings around the edges of the top as we've done here, or use the reserved brownie crumbs from the trimmings across the rest of the top or the sides.

9. Chill the tower in the refrigerator for at least 30 minutes. This firms up the frosting and layers, making them easier to cut.

10. Using a sharp chef's knife, dip the blade into hot water and immediately wipe it completely dry. This is the secret to a clean cut, as the heat melts the chocolate, preventing it from sticking. Make a single, clean cut through the tower. Repeat the "heat and dry" step before each new slice.

Red Velvet Blondie Tower

Using two batches of our blondie base and one batch of our brownie base, and incorporating red velvet–inspired flavors and color (cocoa, red food coloring, cream cheese swirl), I've made a stunning red velvet brownie tower. This is super luxurious and rich, and a little goes a very long way.

SERVES 16

For the red velvet blondie rounds

1 cup plus 7 tbsp (350g) unsalted butter, diced

10oz (300g) white chocolate, broken into small pieces

3 cups (600g) sugar

1 tsp vanilla extract or paste

2¼ cups (300g) all-purpose flour

1 tsp baking powder

4 tbsp cocoa powder

6 eggs

2–4 tsp red food coloring gel or paste

1. Preheat the oven to 350°F (180°C).

2. For the two red velvet blondie rounds, make the blondie batter following steps 2–4 of the White Chocolate Blondie recipe (see p78), adding the cocoa powder to the flour and baking powder at step 3, and adding the red food coloring to the 6 whisked eggs at step 4 (the color should be a uniform, vibrant red).

3. Pour half of the red blondie batter into each of two prepared pans, spreading it evenly over the bases. Bake for 40 minutes. They are done when the edges are set, and the center has risen and started to crack, but may still look a bit soft and jiggly. Test with a toothpick (see step 6, p78). Let cool completely in their pans on a wire rack for 1–2 hours.

4. For the brownie round, follow steps 2–4 of the Original Chocolate Brownie recipe (see p12). Pour the brownie batter into the third prepared pan, spreading it evenly over the base. Bake for 35 minutes (see instructions above to test when they are done). Let cool completely in the pan on a wire rack for 1–2 hours.

5. Meanwhile, make the cream cheese swirl filling and topping. In a medium bowl, use a spatula to beat together the cream cheese and butter until smooth. Sift in the powdered sugar, and beat until fully incorporated and smooth. Stir in the vanilla, if using. Set aside.

6. Once the blondie and brownie rounds have completely cooled, carefully remove them from their pans. If the brownies have sunk in the middle, use a serrated knife (or cake leveler) to trim around the edges to give you a nice flat layer. Reserve for the decoration.

7. To assemble the tower, place one blondie round on a serving plate. Spread one-quarter of the prepared cream cheese mixture evenly over the top of this first layer, using a spatula to spread it to the

YOU WILL NEED

Three 8in (20cm) round baking pans lined with parchment paper
Cake leveler (optional)

recipe continues >>

For the brownie round

¾ cup (175g) unsalted
  butter, diced

3½oz (100g) dark (70%)
  chocolate, broken into
  small pieces

1½ cups (300g) sugar

½ tsp vanilla extract or paste

¾ cup plus 1 tbsp (100g)
  all-purpose flour

½ tsp baking powder

3 eggs

For the cream cheese swirl filling and topping

16oz (550g) full-fat cream
  cheese, at room temperature

1 cup plus 5 tbsp (300g)
  unsalted butter, softened

2½ cups (300g) powdered sugar

1 tsp vanilla extract or paste
  (optional)

edges. Carefully place the brownie round on top of the first blondie layer. Spread another quarter of the cream cheese mixture over the top of the second round.

8. Carefully place the second brownie round on top to make the third layer. Spread the remaining cream cheese swirl mixture evenly over the top and down the sides of the assembled brownie tower, covering it completely. Using the brownie crumbs from the reserved trimmings, decorate the top and sides of the tower.

9. Chill the tower in the refrigerator for at least 30 minutes. This firms up the frosting and layers, making them easier to cut.

10. Once the topping is firm, slice and serve. Using a sharp chef's knife, dip the blade into hot water and immediately wipe it completely dry. This is the secret to a clean cut, as the heat prevents sticking. Make a single, clean cut through the tower. Repeat the "heat and dry" step before each new slice.

Molten Lemon Lava Blondie

Dip a serving spoon into this blondie-based pudding and you get a delicious, lemony-sharp surprise. This zesty and wonderfully messy dessert is perfect served warm.

SERVES 4–6

For the lemon filling

juice and finely grated zest
  of 1½ unwaxed lemons

2½ tbsp cornstarch

⅓ cup (70g) sugar

For the blondie batter

¾ cup (175g) unsalted
  butter, diced

5½oz (150g) white chocolate,
  broken into small pieces

1½ cups (300g) sugar

½ tsp vanilla extract or paste

juice and finely grated zest of
  ½ unwaxed lemon

1¼ cups (150g) all-purpose flour

½ tsp baking powder

3 eggs

1. Begin with the lemon filling. In a bowl, mix the lemon juice and zest and the cornstarch to make a smooth paste. In a separate heatproof bowl, mix the sugar with ⅔ cup (150ml) boiling water until the sugar has completely dissolved. Carefully whisk the hot sugar-water mixture into the lemon-cornstarch paste until well combined and smooth. Set aside.

2. Preheat the oven to 350°F (180°C).

3. Make the blondie batter following steps 2–4 of the White Chocolate Blondie recipe (see p78), adding the lemon juice and zest to the sugar and vanilla at step 3. Pour the prepared blondie batter into a round baking dish, spreading it evenly over the base. Carefully pour the lemon mixture evenly over the top of the blondie batter.

4. Bake for 45–50 minutes. The pudding is done when the edges of the blondie are set and golden brown, and the lemon filling has thickened and is slightly bubbling. Let cool for a few minutes on a wire rack, then serve directly from the dish while the lemon filling is still molten, so that everyone gets a sweet, tangy spoonful of the filling with the warm blondie.

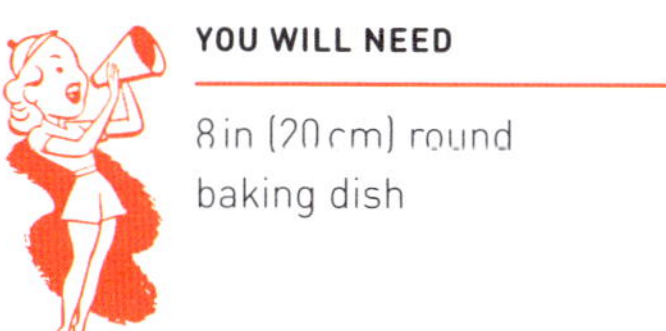

YOU WILL NEED

8in (20cm) round
baking dish

Banana Caramel Blondie

This delightful dessert has the flavors and textures of a classic banoffee pie (named for the thrilling portmanteau of banana and toffee) but with a white chocolate blondie as its base, and topped with a caramel layer, fresh bananas, whipped cream, and chocolate curls.

MAKES 9

¾ cup (175g) unsalted butter, diced

5½oz (150g) white chocolate, broken into small pieces

1½ cups (300g) sugar

½ tsp vanilla extract or paste

1¼ cups (150g) all-purpose flour

½ tsp baking powder

3 eggs

For the banana caramel topping and to decorate

14oz (397g) can caramel or dulce de leche

2–3 medium bananas, chopped

1¼ cups (300ml) heavy cream

3½oz (100g) dark (70%) chocolate, for the chocolate curls

1. Preheat the oven to 350°F (180°C).

2. To make the blondie batter, follow steps 2–4 of the White Chocolate Blondie recipe (see p78).

3. Pour the batter into the prepared pan, spreading it evenly over the base. Bake for 30 minutes. It is done when the edges are set, and the center has risen and started to crack, but may still look a bit soft and jiggly. Test with a toothpick (see step 6, p78).

4. Let the blondie cool completely in the pan on a wire rack for 1–2 hours, or until the bottom of the pan feels cool to the touch. This step is crucial to ensure the blondie is firm enough to support the subsequent layers without becoming soggy or breaking apart.

5. Once the blondie base is completely cool, prepare the topping. Spoon the caramel or dulce de leche evenly over the cooled blondie base, spreading gently to the edges using a palette knife or the back of a spoon. Peel and chop the bananas and arrange them evenly over the caramel layer.

6. In a mixing bowl, whip the cream using a hand whisk until the cream forms soft peaks when the whisk is removed. Take care not to over-whip, as it can easily become too stiff. To assemble, carefully spoon the whipped cream over the chopped bananas, spreading it gently to cover them completely.

7. To decorate, working directly over the blondie, drag a vegetable peeler down the length of the edge of the chocolate bar to create small chocolate curls (you may not need all the chocolate).

8. For best results, chill the blondie in the refrigerator to allow the layers to set. Cut into 9 equal pieces to serve.

YOU WILL NEED

8 x 8 in (20 x 20 cm) square baking pan lined with parchment paper

Lemon Curd Blondie Tower

A total showstopper, and an awful lot easier to make than it looks. This is made by baking our classic blondies into rounds, layering them into a tower, then finishing with a very simple lemon buttercream, and more lemon curd. It will look stunning as a centerpiece on any table, and it will feed an army.

SERVES 18–20

1 cup plus 7 tbsp (350g)
  unsalted butter, diced

zest of 1 unwaxed lemon

10oz (300g) white chocolate,
  broken into small pieces

3 cups (600g) sugar

1 tsp vanilla extract or paste

2¼ cups (300g) all-purpose flour

1 tsp baking powder

6 eggs

**For the buttercream and lemon
curd filling and to decorate**

½ cup plus 2 tbsp (150g)
  unsalted butter, softened

2½ cups (300g) powdered sugar

zest and juice (2–3 tbsp)
  of 1 unwaxed lemon

½ cup (130g) lemon curd

edible flowers, to
  decorate (optional)

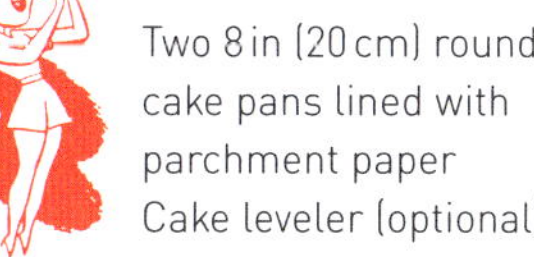

YOU WILL NEED

Two 8in (20cm) round
cake pans lined with
parchment paper
Cake leveler (optional)

1. Preheat the oven to 350ºF (180ºC).

2. For the blondie rounds, make the batter following steps 2–4 of the White Chocolate Blondies recipe (see p78), adding the lemon zest to the butter while it is melting to infuse the flavor at step 2.

3. Divide the batter equally between the two prepared pans, spreading it evenly over the bases. Bake for 30 minutes. They are done when the edges are set, and the center has risen and started to crack, but may still look a bit soft and jiggly. Test with a toothpick (see step 6, p78). Let the blondie rounds cool in their pans for 1–2 hours on a wire rack before removing them from their pans.

4. Meanwhile, for the buttercream, in a medium bowl, use a spatula to beat the butter for 1–2 minutes, until light and fluffy. Sift in the powdered sugar and carefully mix until fully incorporated and smooth. Add the lemon zest and juice, and mix again until you have a well-combined buttercream with a smooth texture.

5. Once the blondie rounds have cooled, if they are uneven or dipped in the middle, you may wish to trim the top using a serrated bread knife or cake leveler (if you have one) to give an even surface.

6. To assemble, place one blondie round on a serving plate. Use a palette knife to spread half of the lemon curd evenly over the top of this first layer. Carefully spread half of the lemon buttercream evenly over the lemon curd layer. Gently place the second blondie round on top of the buttercream layer.

7. Spread the remaining lemon buttercream evenly over the top of the second blondie round, spreading it out to the edges. Spoon over the remaining lemon curd and arrange the edible flowers on top, if you like.

8. Using a sharp chef's knife, dip the blade into hot water and immediately wipe it completely dry. This is the secret to a clean cut, as the heat prevents sticking. Make a single, clean cut through the tower. Repeat the "heat and dry" step before each new slice.

Raspberry and White Chocolate Hot Brownie Pudding

This indulgent recipe transforms the original brownie base into a warm, fruit-filled pudding. With rich, dark chocolate, tangy raspberries, and sweet white chocolate melting into a gooey, squishy center, this is perfect for a cozy dessert.

SERVES 4–6

¾ cup (175g) unsalted butter, diced

3½oz (100g) dark (70%) chocolate, broken into small pieces

1½ cups (300g) sugar

½ tsp vanilla extract or paste

¾ cup plus 1 tbsp (100g) all-purpose flour

½ tsp baking powder

3 eggs

2½oz (75g) raspberries, cut into quarters, plus 8–10 whole raspberries, to decorate

3½oz (100g) white chocolate, broken into chunks

½ cup (50g) chopped hazelnuts (optional)

ice cream, to serve

1. Preheat the oven to 350°F (180°C).

2. For the brownie pudding base, make the brownie batter following steps 2–4 of the Original Chocolate Brownie recipe (see p12). At the end of step 4, carefully mix the quartered raspberries and the white chocolate chunks into the brownie batter, being very gentle to prevent the white chocolate from melting before baking.

3. Pour the batter into the prepared skillet. Gently push the 8–10 whole raspberries into the surface of the brownie, then scatter over the hazelnuts, if using. Bake for 50–55 minutes. The edges should be a bit crusty and firm to the touch, while the middle will be molten and runny.

4. Let the brownie cool in the skillet for 10–15 minutes once baked. Serve still warm directly from the skillet, adding scoops of ice cream of your choice.

YOU WILL NEED

8 in (20 cm) skillet or oven-safe dish lined with parchment paper

Coffee and Walnut Brownie Tower

This has been one of our best-selling brownie flavors for years, so it seemed only right to give it the kudos it deserves. Here, we've turned it into its own fabulous dessert tower, topped with a sweet yet subtle coffee buttercream.

SERVES 16

1 cup plus 7 tbsp (350g) unsalted butter, diced

7oz (200g) dark (70%) chocolate, broken into small pieces

3 cups (600g) sugar

1 tsp vanilla extract or paste

1½ cups (200g) all-purpose flour

1 tsp baking powder

3 tbsp instant espresso powder

6 eggs

¾ cup (75g) chopped walnuts, plus ¼ cup (25g) walnut halves, for decoration

For the coffee buttercream

½ cup plus 2 tbsp (150g) unsalted butter, softened

2½ cups (300g) powdered sugar

2 tbsp instant espresso powder

3–4 tbsp milk

1 tsp vanilla extract or paste

¼ cup (25g) chopped walnuts (optional)

YOU WILL NEED

Two 8in (20cm) round baking pans lined with parchment paper

1. Preheat the oven to 350°F (180°C).

2. For the brownie rounds, make the batter following steps 2–4 of the Original Chocolate Brownie recipe (see p12), adding the espresso powder along with the flour and baking powder at step 3. Gently fold in the ¾ cup (75g) of chopped walnuts at step 4 until just combined.

3. Divide the batter equally between the two prepared baking pans, spreading it evenly over the bases. Bake for 30–35 minutes. They are done when the edges are set, and the center has risen and started to crack, but may still look a bit soft and jiggly. Test with a toothpick (see step 6, p12). Let the brownie rounds cool on a wire rack for 1–2 hours before removing them from the pans.

4. Meanwhile, for the coffee buttercream, in a medium bowl, use a spatula to beat the butter for 2–3 minutes until light and fluffy. Sift in the powdered sugar and espresso powder, and mix until fully incorporated and smooth. Add the milk and vanilla (and the ¼ cup/25g of chopped walnuts, if using), and mix again until smooth, with a good spreading consistency.

5. To assemble the tower, put one brownie round on a cake stand or serving plate. Using a palette knife, spread half of the coffee buttercream evenly over the top of this first round. Carefully place the second brownie round on top of the buttercream layer.

6. Spread the remaining coffee buttercream evenly over the top of the tower, spreading it right to the edges. Decorate with the walnut halves, if using.

7. Let the buttercream set before slicing. Using a sharp chef's knife, dip the blade into hot water and immediately wipe it completely dry. This is the secret to a clean cut, as the heat prevents sticking. Make a single, clean cut through the tower. Repeat the "heat and dry" step before each new slice.

BEYOND BROWNIES

Diwali Blondie

Warming Diwali-inspired spices and nuts are the inspiration for this blondie, and it's topped with a delicate buttercream frosting flavored with cardamom and rose water.

MAKES 9

¾ cup (175g) unsalted butter, diced

5½oz (150g) white chocolate, broken into small pieces

1½ cups (300g) sugar

½ tsp vanilla extract or paste

1¼ cups (150g) all-purpose flour

½ tsp baking powder

½ cup (45g) ground almonds

¼ tsp ground cinnamon

¼ tsp ground cardamom

3 eggs

⅓ cup (45g) chopped unsalted pistachios, plus extra to serve

For the buttercream

6½ tbsp (100g) unsalted butter, softened

1 tsp vanilla extract or paste

½ tsp ground cardamom

½ tsp rose water

scant 1 cup (200g) sweetened condensed milk

To decorate

your choice of edible dried rose petals, glitter, and/or gold leaf

1. Preheat the oven to 350°F (180°C).

2. To make the blondie batter, follow steps 2–3 of the White Chocolate Blondie recipe (see p78). At step 3, mix the flour, baking powder, ground almonds, cinnamon, and cardamom together in a bowl before adding to the wet ingredients. Mix until no lumps of flour or sugar are visible.

3. In a medium bowl, whisk the eggs for 20–30 seconds until light and frothy. Using a large metal spoon, carefully fold the whisked eggs through the chocolate mixture, keeping as much air in the mixture as possible, to form a thick, smooth batter. Gently fold in the chopped pistachios until just combined. Pour the batter into the prepared pan, spreading it evenly over the base.

4. Bake for 35–40 minutes. Test with a toothpick (see step 6, p78). Let cool completely in the pan on a wire rack for 1–2 hours. Cooling completely is crucial for clean slices.

5. For the buttercream, in a mixing bowl, use an electric hand whisk on high speed to beat the butter for 1–2 minutes until it is pale and silky. Add the vanilla, cardamom, and rose water and mix. With the mixer running at medium speed, gradually add the sweetened condensed milk and continue mixing until the buttercream is light, smooth, and fluffy.

6. Once the blondie is completely cool, spread the buttercream evenly over the blondie using a palette knife. Finish with chopped pistachios and decorations of your choice. Slice into 9 equal pieces and serve.

YOU WILL NEED

8 x 8 in (20 x 20 cm) square baking pan lined with parchment paper
Electric hand whisk

Cinnamon Brownie Roll

This satisfying centerpiece is our classic brownie re-imagined as a cinnamon roll, topped with that drizzle of icing. The buttercream filling is your tastiest friend here, and will fill in any cracks that may occur during rolling.

SERVES 8

¾ cup (175g) unsalted
    butter, diced

3½oz (100g) dark (70%)
    chocolate, broken into
    small pieces

1½ cups (300g) sugar

½ tsp vanilla extract or paste

¾ cup plus 1 tbsp (100g)
    all-purpose flour

½ tsp baking powder

3 eggs

For the cinnamon buttercream

5 tbsp (70g) unsalted
    butter, softened

1⅔ cups (200g) powdered sugar

1 tbsp milk

2 tsp ground cinnamon

1. Preheat the oven to 350°F (180°C).

2. To make the brownie batter, follow steps 2–4 of the Original Chocolate Brownie recipe (see p12). Pour the batter into the prepared pan, spreading it evenly over the base. Bake for 20 minutes.

3. Lay a sheet of parchment paper (or a clean dish towel) on a work surface. When the brownie has finished baking, tip it onto the parchment and peel off the lining paper.

4. Let cool for 5 minutes, then, working quickly while it's still hot, roll the brownie up from the short edge with the paper (or dish towel) inside. The brownie must be shaped into a roll while it is still warm and pliable. Let the rolled brownie cool completely, for at least 4–6 hours.

5. Meanwhile, make the cinnamon buttercream. In a bowl, use a spatula to beat the butter until smooth. Sift in the powdered sugar, adding it gradually, mixing between additions, until fully incorporated and smooth. Add the milk and cinnamon, then mix again until the buttercream is smooth and creamy.

recipe continues >>

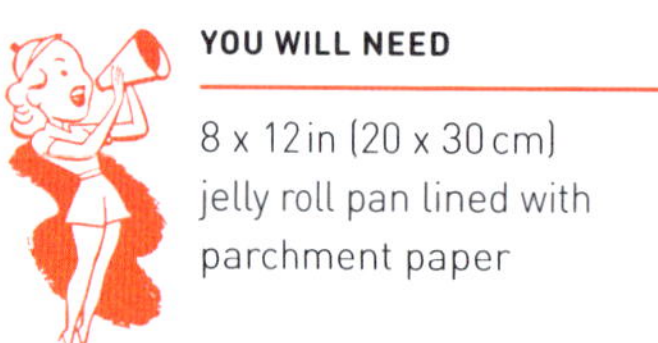

YOU WILL NEED

8 x 12in (20 x 30cm)
jelly roll pan lined with
parchment paper

For the simple drizzle icing

2 tbsp powdered sugar

To serve

1 tbsp sugar

2 tsp ground cinnamon

6. Gently unroll the cooled brownie. Use a palette knife to spread a thick layer of the cinnamon buttercream evenly over the surface of each piece. Reassemble the log from the cracked pieces, using the buttercream as a glue to hold it together, and re-form it to the original log shape. Put the assembled log on the jelly roll pan and chill in the refrigerator for 30 minutes.

7. For the simple drizzle icing, in a small bowl, mix the powdered sugar and 1 teaspoon of water, adding the water gradually until you have a liquid mixture.

8. Remove the log from the refrigerator. Drizzle half of the icing over the finished log, reserving the remainder for serving.

9. Cut the cinnamon log into 8 even slices, then arrange the slices on a plate. To serve, combine the sugar and cinnamon to make the cinnamon sugar. Sprinkle the arranged slices with the cinnamon sugar and finish with a final drizzle of the remaining icing.

Double Chocolate Brownie Tower

This recipe is for the chocoholics in your life. Pure, unadulterated chocolate through and through, right up to the chocolate shavings on the top. It also makes an excellent Christmas centerpiece.

SERVES 9–12

1 cup plus 7 tbsp (350g)
  unsalted butter, diced

7oz (200g) dark (70%) chocolate,
  broken into small pieces

3 cups (600g) sugar

1 tsp vanilla extract or paste

1½ cups (200g) all-purpose flour

1 tsp baking powder

6 eggs

¼ cup chocolate shavings

For the chocolate buttercream

½ cup plus 2 tbsp (150g)
  unsalted butter, softened

2½ cups (300g) powdered sugar

1 cup (80g) good-quality
  cocoa powder

3–4 tbsp milk

1 tsp vanilla extract or paste

1. Preheat the oven to 350°F (180°C).

2. For the brownie rounds, make the brownie batter following steps 2–4 of the Original Chocolate Brownie recipe (see p12).

3. Divide the batter equally between the prepared baking pans, spreading it evenly over the bases. Bake for 30–35 minutes. They are done when the edges are set, and the center has risen and started to crack, but may still look a bit soft and jiggly. Test with a toothpick (see step 6, p12).

4. Let the brownie rounds cool in their pans on a wire rack for 1–2 hours before removing them from the pans.

5. Meanwhile, for the chocolate buttercream, in a medium bowl, use a spatula to beat the butter for 1–2 minutes until light and fluffy. Sift in the powdered sugar and cocoa powder and carefully mix until fully incorporated and smooth. Add the milk and vanilla, and mix until the buttercream is smooth, with a good spreading consistency.

6. To assemble the tower, put one brownie round on a cake board or serving plate. Using a palette knife, carefully spread half of the chocolate buttercream evenly over the top of the first round. Gently place the second brownie round on top of the chocolate buttercream layer.

7. Spread the remaining chocolate buttercream over the top of the tower, spreading it right to the edges. Sprinkle the chocolate shavings over the top to decorate.

8. Using a sharp chef's knife, dip the blade into hot water and immediately wipe it completely dry. This is the secret to a clean cut, as the heat melts the chocolate, preventing it from sticking. Make a single, clean cut through the tower. Repeat the "heat and dry" step before each new slice.

YOU WILL NEED

Two 8in (20cm) round baking pans lined with parchment paper

Brownie Christmas Pudding

Mincemeat, a British treat with dried fruit and spices, transforms the rich, gooey chocolate brownie base into something deliciously festive. It then gets a long, gentle steaming, and the result is a dense, moist, chocolatey brownie reminiscent of a Christmas plum pudding.

SERVES 8

¾ cup (175g) unsalted butter, diced, plus extra to grease

3½oz (100g) dark (70%) chocolate, broken into small pieces

1½ cups (300g) sugar

½ tsp vanilla extract or paste

¾ cup plus 1 tbsp (100g) all-purpose flour

½ tsp baking powder

3 eggs

14oz (400g) jar mincemeat

ice cream or hard sauce, to serve

YOU WILL NEED

1 large pudding basin, about 2½-pint (1.4-liter) capacity
Large saucepan or steamer with a lid
Parchment paper and aluminum foil
Kitchen string

1. Thoroughly grease the pudding basin with butter. Place an old saucer or trivet on the bottom of a large, heavy-based, lidded saucepan suitable for steaming. Fill the saucepan one-quarter full with water and bring it to a boil.

2. To make the brownie batter, follow steps 2–4 of the Original Chocolate Brownie recipe (see p12). At the end of step 4, gently fold the mincemeat thoroughly into the prepared brownie batter until evenly distributed.

3. Spoon the mixture into the prepared pudding basin, leaving a space of around 1 in (2.5 cm) at the top of the bowl to allow for rising. Cut a round of parchment paper that will sit directly on the surface of the brownie batter. Take a sheet of aluminum foil and make a pleat in the middle, about 1 in (2.5 cm) wide. This will allow the foil to accommodate the pudding's rise as it cooks. Cover the basin with the parchment paper and pleated foil, then wrap the whole basin tightly in foil to ensure it is watertight. Use plenty of kitchen string to securely tie the foil under the lip of the basin, using extra string to create a handle.

4. Once the water in your saucepan is boiling, use the handle to place the basin gently into the saucepan, ensuring the water comes three-quarters of the way up the sides of the basin. Cover the saucepan with the lid, turn the heat to low-medium to maintain a gentle boil, and steam for 3 hours and 15 minutes. As it steams, regularly check the water level and add more boiling water, if necessary, to prevent the pudding from boiling dry.

5. Once cooked, let the pudding cool completely for 3–4 hours. To remove it from the basin, gently run a knife between the brownie pudding and the bowl to loosen, then carefully turn it upside down into a serving dish, allowing the pudding to drop out.

6. When ready to serve, you can warm the pudding gently in the microwave for 30 seconds to 1 minute. Serve with a few dollops of ice cream or hard sauce.

Chestnut Brownie Yule Log

I've used our basic brownie recipe to create a thin, rollable slab that makes a beautiful and festive Yule log. The chestnut buttercream is crucial for reassembling the log if the baked brownie sheet cracks when unrolled—a highly likely event!

SERVES 8–10

¾ cup (175g) unsalted butter, diced

3½oz (100g) dark (70%) chocolate, broken into small pieces

1½ cups (300g) sugar

½ tsp vanilla extract or paste

¾ cup plus 1 tbsp (100g) all-purpose flour

½ tsp baking powder

3 eggs

For the chestnut buttercream

5 tbsp plus 1 tsp (80g) unsalted butter, softened

3½oz (100g) chestnut puree

1 tbsp heavy cream

1 cup (120g) powdered sugar, sifted, plus extra to decorate

1. Preheat the oven to 350°F (180°C).

2. To make the brownie batter, follow steps 2–4 of the Original Chocolate Brownie recipe (see p12). Pour the batter into the prepared pan, using a spatula to spread it evenly over the base. Bake for 20 minutes.

3. Lay a sheet of parchment paper (or a clean dish towel) on a work surface. When the brownie has finished baking, tip it onto the parchment and peel off the lining paper. Let cool for 5 minutes, then, working quickly while it's still hot, roll the brownie up from the short edge with the paper (or dish towel) inside. The brownie must be shaped into a roll while it is still warm and pliable. Let the rolled brownie cool completely, for at least 4–6 hours.

4. Meanwhile, make the chestnut buttercream. In a bowl, use a spatula to beat the butter until smooth, then mix in the chestnut puree and the cream, and mix until smooth. Add the powdered sugar gradually, 1 tablespoon at a time, mixing until fully incorporated, and the buttercream is smooth and creamy.

5. Gently unroll the cooled brownie. When unrolled, the brownie is very likely to crack and break, but don't worry, you can easily reassemble it. Use a palette knife to spread a thick layer of the chestnut buttercream on each of the pieces, then reassemble the log from the cracked pieces using the buttercream as a glue to hold it together, re-forming it into the original log shape.

6. Put the assembled log on the jelly roll pan and chill in the refrigerator for 30 minutes. Chilling the brownie helps the filling set and stabilizes the structure before frosting.

recipe continues >>

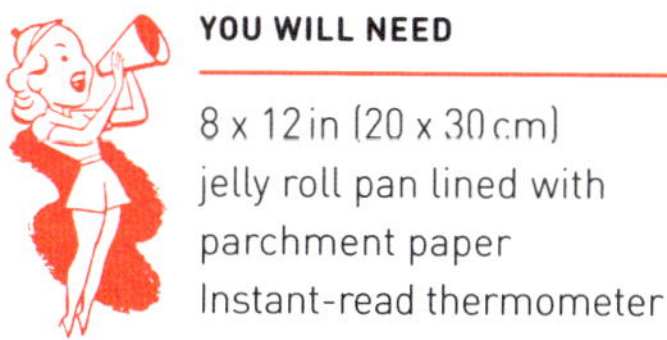

YOU WILL NEED

8 x 12 in (20 x 30 cm) jelly roll pan lined with parchment paper
Instant-read thermometer

For the chocolate ganache

¼ cup (50ml) heavy cream

3½oz (100g) dark (at least 50%)
chocolate, broken into
small pieces

7. For the chocolate ganache, put the chocolate in a heatproof bowl.
   Heat the cream in a pan or microwave until it reaches 194°F (90°C),
   just below boiling, then pour the hot cream over the dark chocolate.
   Let stand for 2–3 minutes, then use a spatula to mix thoroughly
   until smooth.

8. Remove the log from the refrigerator. If you like, you can slice a
   bit off the ends to even out the log and make it neater. Cut a thick
   diagonal slice from one end and arrange it on the side with the
   diagonal cut against the brownie to make a branch.

9. Using a palette knife, spread the chocolate ganache evenly over
   the entire log and any branch pieces (do not cover the cut ends).
   The ganache frosting will help to cover and fill up any cracks
   and splits.

10. Use the tines of a fork or a butter knife to give the ganache the effect
    of tree bark. Think about how a tree grows, ensuring the lines
    follow the direction of the log and branches. Scatter over some
    powdered sugar to resemble snow, and serve.

Celebration Brownie Tower

This recipe creates two rich, deeply festive brownie rounds infused with mincemeat, stacked high, and sealed with chocolate buttercream, golden marzipan, and a final layer of fondant icing for a classic Christmas finish. With a few strategic decoration adjustments, this brownie tower could become a wedding cake, christening cake, or even a cake to celebrate Easter—a four-in-one celebratory brownie.

SERVES 16

1 cup plus 7 tbsp (350g) unsalted butter, diced

7oz (200g) dark (70%) chocolate, broken into small pieces

3 cups (600g) sugar

1 tsp vanilla extract or paste

1½ cups (200g) all-purpose flour

1 tsp baking powder

6 eggs

14oz (400g) jar mincemeat

For the chocolate buttercream filling

4 tbsp (50g) unsalted butter, softened

scant 1 cup (100g) powdered sugar, plus extra to dust

⅓ cup (30g) good-quality cocoa powder

1 tbsp milk

½ tsp vanilla extract or paste

1. Preheat the oven to 350°F (180°C).

2. For the brownie rounds, make the brownie batter following steps 2–4 of the Original Chocolate Brownie recipe (see p12). At the end of step 4, gently fold the mincemeat into the batter until evenly distributed.

3. Divide the batter evenly between the two prepared baking pans. Bake for 35–40 minutes. They are done when the edges are set, and the center has risen and started to crack, but may still look a bit soft and jiggly.

4. Test with a toothpick (see step 6, p12). Once baked, let both brownie rounds cool completely for 1–2 hours before turning out.

5. For the chocolate buttercream, in a bowl, use a spatula to beat the softened butter for 2–3 minutes, until light and fluffy. Sift in the powdered sugar and cocoa powder, then carefully mix until fully incorporated and smooth. Add the milk and vanilla, then mix until smooth.

6. To assemble and decorate the tower, if the brownie rounds are uneven or dipped in the middle, you may wish to trim the tops using a serrated knife or cake leveler, if you have one. Place one cooled brownie round on a cake stand or serving plate. Using a palette knife, spread the buttercream evenly over the top of this first round. Carefully place the second brownie round on top of the icing layer. Gently warm the apricot jam in the microwave to make it easy to spread. Using a pastry brush, spread a thin layer of jam over the whole brownie tower to help the marzipan stick.

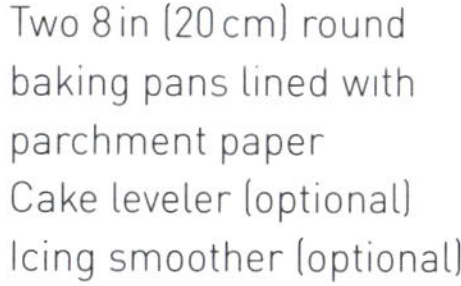

YOU WILL NEED

Two 8in (20cm) round baking pans lined with parchment paper
Cake leveler (optional)
Icing smoother (optional)

recipe continues >>

To assemble

2–3 tbsp apricot jam

2¼lb (1kg) ready-made
golden marzipan

2¼lb (1kg) ready-made
fondant icing

7. Knead the marzipan on a work surface until soft and pliable.
   Lightly dust your work surface with powdered sugar, then roll out
   the marzipan to an even thickness of around ¼in (5mm). Using the
   rolling pin to help you, gently lift and drape the marzipan over the
   tower. Use the palms of your hands to slowly smooth the marzipan
   onto the top and down the sides, molding it into place. Trim off the
   excess marzipan neatly from the base.

8. Roll out the ready-made fondant icing to an even thickness around
   ¼in (5mm). Using the rolling pin, gently lift and drape the fondant
   icing over the marzipan-covered tower. Use the palms of your
   hands to mold the icing smoothly. Trim off the excess icing from
   the base and use an icing smoother or the palms of your hands
   to bring out a final natural sheen on the icing.

9. Your brownie tower is now ready to decorate (see facing page).

10. To serve, using a sharp chef's knife, dip the blade into hot water
    and immediately wipe it completely dry. This is the secret to a
    clean cut, as the heat melts the layers, preventing sticking. Make
    a single, clean cut through the tower. Repeat the "heat and dry"
    step before each new slice.

pictured overleaf >>

CHRISTMAS DECORATIONS

- Apply small, delicate flakes of edible gold or silver leaf across the top and down the sides.

- Line the base of the cake with a single, neat border of silver edible pearls, or scatter them lightly on top like tiny jewels.

- Secure a wide, beautiful ribbon (velvet, satin, or metallic organza) in a contrasting color, such as deep red, emerald green, or gold, around the base.

- Use a classic holly leaf cutter (or make the leaves by hand) from green fondant and roll tiny red fondant balls for berries.

EASTER DECORATIONS

- Roll balls of marzipan into egg shapes and place on top along with fresh edible flowers, and chocolate chicks or bunnies.

- Create a "nest" in the center with a few sprigs of bay leaves or edible leaves and fill it with a small pile of mini speckled chocolate eggs.

WEDDING DECORATIONS

- Delicate, realistic sugar flowers are a classic. They can be arranged in cascades down the side of the tiers, as a cluster on top, or circling the base of each tier.

- Perfectly smooth, sharp-edged fondant with little to no additional decoration. The beauty is in the flawless execution.

CHRISTENING DECORATIONS

- While the cake is primarily white fondant, a subtle accent color helps to personalize it.

- Pale pink, blue, lilac, or peach accents can be used for ribbons, sugar flowers, edible pearls, or the base trim of the cake.

- Soft sage green or a touch of gold or silver gives an elegant, modern feel.

Index

Page numbers in **bold** refer to photographs

A

almond
    Diwali blondie **138**, 139
    honey toffee and almond brownie 60–1
    orange and almond brownie 55
    pink almond blondie 40–2, **41**
    sugar-free brownie 16
    white chocolate Bakewell blondie 94, **95**
apple
    apple crumble and custard blondie 86–7, **88–9**
    caramel apple upside-down blondie 96
Armagnac, far Breton blondie 103, **104–5**

B

bacon maple pecan brownie **20**, 21
Bakewell blondie 94, **95**
banana caramel blondie 130, **131**
Battenberg brownie 40–2, **41**
birthday blondie tower **120**, 121
Black Forest brownie tower **116**, 117
blondie towers
    birthday **120**, 121
    jam and cream 118, **119**
    lemon curd **132**, 133
    red velvet 125–6, **127**
blondies 77–113
    apple crumble and custard 86–7, **88–9**
    banana caramel 130, **131**
    caramel apple upside-down 96
    carrot cake 100–2, **101**
    Diwali **138**, 139
    Dubai chocolate pistachio **106**, 107
    far Breton 103, **104–5**
    gluten-free 82
    hot skillet 79
    jam and coconut **90**, 91
    lemon meringue pie 110–11, **112–13**
    matcha 83, **84–5**
    molten lemon lava **128**, 129
    peanut butter and jelly 92, **93**
    pink almond 40–2, **41**

Valentine's 108, **109**
    white chocolate 78
    white chocolate Bakewell 94, **95**
brittle, honey toffee 60–1
brownie towers
    Black Forest **116**, 117
    Christmas 149–51, **152–3**
    coffee and walnut 136, **137**
    death by chocolate 122, **123–4**
    double chocolate 143
brownies 11–75
    bacon maple pecan **20**, 21
    Battenberg **41**, 42
    bitter orange marmalade 28
    brownie Christmas pudding 144, **145**
    brownie mince pies **70**, 71
    burnt Basque cheesecake 56–7, **58–9**
    chestnut brownie Yule log **146**, 147–8
    chili chocolate 26
    cinnamon brownie roll 140–2, **141**
    cookie dough 47, **48–9**
    fruit and nut granola bar 68, **69**
    ginger drizzle 27
    gluten-free 17
    Halloween spiced latte 72, **73**
    honey toffee and almond 60–1
    hot skillet 13
    key lime pie **62**, 63–4
    maple pecan **20**, 21
    mint choc chip 18, **19**
    nut butter swirl 22
    orange and almond 55
    original chocolate 12
    peanut butter salted caramel 23, **24–5**
    pear and hazelnut 65
    pineapple and coconut upside-down 50, **51**
    raspberry and white chocolate hot brownie pudding 134, **135**
    raspberry ripple **38**, 39
    rhubarb crumble and custard 34–5, **37**
    rum and raisin **32**, 33
    St. Patrick's Day 66, **67**
    sticky toffee **52**, 53–4
    strawberries and cream 43
    sugar free 16
    toffee crisp **44**, 45
    Welsh cake **74**, 75

burnt Basque cheesecake brownie 56–7, **58–9**
butter
    butter infusion 29, **30**
    chestnut **146**, 147–8
    cinnamon 140–2, **141**
buttercream 122, **123–4**, **138**, 139
    coffee 29, **30**, 136, **137**
    Irish cream 143, 149–51, **152–3**
    lemon **132**, 133
    pumpkin 72, **73**
    rum and raisin **32**, 33
    vanilla 108, **109**, 118, **119**, **120**, 121

C

caramel
    banana caramel blondie 130, **131**
    caramel apple upside-down blondie 96
    peanut butter salted caramel brownie 23, **24–5**
    salted caramel sauce 23, **24–5**, 79
carrot cake blondie 100–2, **101**
celebrations 115–53
celebration brownie tower 149–51, **152–3**
cheesecake
    burnt Basque cheesecake brownie 56–7, **58–9**
cherry
    Black Forest brownie tower **116**, 117
    dark cherries in syrup, boozy 79
    pineapple and coconut upside-down brownie 50, **51**
chestnut brownie Yule log **146**, 147–8
chili chocolate brownie 26
chocolate chip
    cookie dough brownie 47, **48–9**
    mint choc chip brownie 18, **19**
chocolate (dark)
    bacon maple pecan brownie **20**, 21
    Battenberg brownie 40–2, **41**
    bitter orange marmalade brownie 28
    Black Forest brownie tower **116**, 117
    banana caramel blondie 130, **131**
    brownie mince pies **70**, 71
    burnt Basque cheesecake brownie 56–7, **58–9**
    chestnut brownie Yule log **146**, 147–8

Acknowledgments

Thank you, thank you, thank you…

To the person that kicked this all off, Stephanie Jackson, publisher extraordinaire, to have such unwavering faith in me and for all your friendship over the years, I am so truly thankful.

To the incredible team at DK, especially Cara Armstrong and Lucy Sienkowska, you held my hand throughout a process that was totally out of my comfort zone. I am so grateful for your expert advice and unbelievable patience.

To my twinnie, Anita Mangan, it was a dream come true that we were actually able to work together. I'm so lucky to have you as a friend. For all the amazing graphics and illustrations. The care and attention you gave to the design of this book was never ending. I love how you always have my back.

To Susan Low, for your great eye for detail on the recipe editing. Kim Lightbody for the beautiful photographs, Tabitha Hawkins for prop styling, and super food stylist, Holly Cochrane, for the sheer hard graft.

To my lovely friend Scarlet Page for my gorgeous author picture, the only person who can actually make me relax, smile, and laugh in front of a camera.

To all the elves back at the Brownie Barns who work so hard to keep those brownies rolling out across the country and allow me the opportunity to be able to take the time out to create this book. Best team ever!

To my fantastic customers, many of whom have supported me from day one. Your loyalty over the years has always made my job so worthwhile. The stories you have shared of how my brownies have become part of your family celebrations, traditions, and even your go-to during the tough times, have always been so utterly heartwarming. Thank you.

And, finally, to my brilliant Rob. You and I have proved ourselves as the ultimate Dream Team. Gower Cottage Brownies wouldn't be what it is now without you at the helm, letting me run with my crazy idea of setting up a little business selling brownies as gifts online. I've never forgotten in the early days when you said, "You go and do what you do and I'll make sure it happens." You've never swayed from this extraordinary support, and are a logistical genius.

Kate

X

About the Author

Kate Jenkins, the creative force behind Gower Cottage Brownies, has built a reputation for crafting some of the most indulgent and beloved brownies in the UK. What began in 2007, supplying the local village shop from her home kitchen in Gower Cottage, has blossomed into a thriving business. Now, nearly 20 years later, Kate sends out hundreds of gift boxes daily from the picturesque Brownie Barns in Reynoldston, Gower, in South Wales. Kate is known for her commitment to quality, sustainability, and local sourcing, and her brownies have become a symbol of heartfelt gifting and culinary excellence. In her spare time, Kate contributes to the Welsh food industry as a board member of the Abergavenny Food Festival, using her expertise to guide its growth. She has appeared on BBC's *Saturday Kitchen* and ITV's *This Morning*.

@gowercottage

www.gowercottagebrownies.co.uk

DK LONDON
Editorial Director Cara Armstrong
Senior Editor Lucy Sienkowska
Americanization Editor Sharon Lucas
US Executive Editor Lori Cates Hand
Design Manager Tania Gomes
DTP and Design Coordinator Heather Blagden
Senior Production Controller Stephanie McConnell
Art Director Maxine Pedliham
Publishing Director Stephanie Jackson

Design and Art Direction Anita Mangan
Photography Kim Lightbody
Portrait Photography Scarlet Page
Prop Styling Tabitha Hawkins
Food Styling Holly Cochrane
Editorial Susan Low

DK DELHI
Senior Art Editor Ira Sharma
Managing Art Editor Neha Ahuja Chowdhry
Production Designer Manish Upreti, Satish Gaur
Production Editor Pushpak Tyagi
Production Manager Balwant Singh
Creative Head Malavika Talukder

First American Edition, 2026
Published in the United States by DK Publishing,
a division of Penguin Random House LLC
1745 Broadway, 20th Floor, New York, NY 10019

Printed and bound in China

www.dk.com

This book was made with Forest
Stewardship Council™ certified
paper—one small step in DK's
commitment to a sustainable future.
**Learn more at www.dk.com/uk/
information/sustainability**

PUBLISHER'S ACKNOWLEDGMENTS
Dorling Kindersley would like to thank Jordan
Lambley for design assistance, Katie Hardwicke
for proofreading, Lisa Footitt for providing the
index, and Renee Wilmeth for consulting on
the US edition.